GIFTED ACHIEVERS AND UNDERACHIEVERS

—AN APPRAISAL

GIFTED ACHIEVERS AND UNDERACHIEVERS

— *AN APPRAISAL*

By

Dr. Mahmood Ahmad Khan

Department of Education
University of Kashmir
Srinagar

DISCOVERY PUBLISHING HOUSE
NEW DELHI-110002

Reprinted - 2019

First Published - 2005

ISBN: 978-81-8356-043-6

Gifted Achievers & Underachievers - An Appraisal

Published by:

DISCOVERY PUBLISHING HOUSE PVT. LTD.
4383/4B, Ansari Road, Darya Ganj
New Delhi-110 002 (India)
Phone: +91-11-23279245, 23253475; 43596065
E-mail: discoverybooksindia@gmail.com
discoverypublishinghouse@gmail.com
web: www.discoverypublishinggroup.com

Printed at:
Infinity Imaging Systems
Delhi

Faculty of Education
UNIVERSITY OF DELHI

Department of Education
(CENTRAL INSTITUTE OF EDUCATION)
33 Chhatra Marg, New Delhi-110007
Tel: 27666377, 27667030, 27667509
Telefax: 27667925
Email: cieidu@nda.vsnl.net.in
Internet: www.cie.du.ac.in

Foreword

It is a pleasure to write about a book which deals with a subject that is very close to my heart. Dr. Mahmood Ahmad Khan in his book titled *'Gifted Achievers and Underachievers – An Appraisal'* has completed an unfinished job done on gifted underachievers in India as studies done here hardly focused on gifted children from rural and remote areas of our country. His contribution in this regard should be highlighted as this study took shape in the back-drop of rural Kashmir. I want to praise his effort for Urdu adaptation of HSPQ (Cattell, 1976), Need Achievement, ISB, (Mukherjee, 1968) and Kashmiri adaptation of socioeconomic status scale, rural (Pareek and Trivedi, 1964). Very few authors in this area have used such rigorous statistical techniques as have been used by Dr. Khan. The profiles of both the gifted achievers and underachievers have clearly posited the fact that the rural gifted are no way different from the so-called urban gifted though SES factor can not be ignored. I hope that Dr. Khan will pursue his research on gifted children for discovering many other important facts that are yet to come to light. For teacher-educators particularly those who are involved in training of school teachers should be initiated to this book, not only for its academic flavour but also for the cause of the gifted children, who need our constant encouragement and motivation to realize their talents and to prevent themselves from the onslaught of underachievement or its syndrome.

Prof. Krishna Maitra

Preface

To attain the objective of self reliance in any field of inquiry, every society needs highly capable personnel who are not only able to maintain but also to evolve alternative strategies with given resources and replace the outdated technology with a more efficient one. To answer this demand, even Plato in his *Republic* was inspired to plead the case of special mental abilities to hold the charge of his ideal state. Terman showed interest for the gifted and conducted studies on this precious human resource.

India is already facing the highest illiteracy rate wastage and stagnation and above all brain drain. Therefore, it becomes more pertinent to care for the talented. Due to underachievement, the gifted get lost among the millions, even for that matter they become social deviants or continue as laggers.

A high intelligence goes with high scholastic achievement is a fact that is well established. The author got baffled with the fact that about 50 percent of bright subjects in rural Kashmir are underachievers (Lidhoo and Khan, 1990). As against this, in England the corresponding position is 25 percent (Whitemore 1980). Children are not born underachievers their school behaviour is acquired (Davis and Rim, 1985). And fortunately, as the authors experience has shown, the teachers can be very effective in helping underachieving children if and only if they are aware about their personal endowments. The author got interested in the field and tried his level best to find out the characteristic features of the gifted achievers and underachievers with special reference to personality, need achievement and socio-economic status. The author has also developed factor based profile associated with gifted achievers and underachievers by analysing 21 variables.

In this book the author discusses the problems of gifted underachievers. He has substantiated his discussion by empirical data collected on a sample of gifted achievers and underachievers selected from the Government schools of rural population of Kashmir, who are otherwise at a disadvantage. The book presents a cognitive map of the specific characteristic features of gifted achievers and underachievers. The book is of practical use to teachers at all levels of education - pre-primary to University, counsellors, educational administrators, social workers, parents and teacher trainees. The book will help in identifying most recurring profiles of gifted achievers and underachievers and develop a strategic measure to nourish and uplift giftedness in children. The book will go a long way in identifying and rehabilitating the gifted underachievers.

Prof. M. L. Lidhoo and Prof. A. G. Madhosh, (former Dean and Head, Faculty of Education), my philosopher friends, affectionate teachers deserve thanks much beyond the scope of my poor vocabulary. Their sincere supervision, painstaking and erudite suggestions, parental temperament and affection and intellectual stimulation has enabled me to complete this book with enthusiasm.

I have been benefited immensely while pursuing the book at various stages by eminent scholars at national level. Among these Prof. Baqir Mehdi and Prof. M.K Raina, NCERT; Prof. Vidhu Mohan, Punjab University; the Late Prof. G. Rasool of Jammu University and Prof. Mohd Mian,

Jamia Millia Islamia, deserve cordial thanks on my behalf. Their valuable suggestions have added richness to this book.

I am especially grateful to Prof. Krishna Maitra, Faculty of Education, University of Delhi, who very kindly wrote a foreword to this volume. Thanks are also due to Prof. G. R. Malik, Department of Engish, for going through an earlier draft of the book and making some useful suggestions. I am also thankful to my teachers, Prof Agha Ashraf Ali, Prof. C. L. Vishan, Dr. A. H. Zargar and colleagues. Prof. G. M. Malik, Dean Faculty of Education, Prof. N. A. Nadeem, Prof. A. R. Rather, Dr. M. Y. Ganai, Dr. M. I. Mattoo, Dr. Tasleema for their cooperation and encouragement. My sincere thanks are due to Dr. B. S. Nagi, Council for Social Development, New Delhi for computerization of the data.

The contribution of my parents, Haji Gh. Ahmad Khan and Mrs. Sara Begum, wife, Farhat Habib and Brother Er. Ali Mohd. Khan is worth mentioning. Their affection, care and cooperation enabled me to complete the book in time. M/s Computer Vision, Sadurbal, Srinagar also deserve thanks for typing the manuscript with meticulous care. I am indebted to M/s Discovery Publications, New Delhi for publishing this book with all care.

Dr. Mahmood Ahmad Khan

Srinagar-190006
Tel: 0194-2423679
Mobile: 9419075938
Email: drmahmood1962@yahoo.co.in

Contents

Contents

Introduction

Research is perhaps the only assurance we have that a discipline or a profession will not decay into meaningless scraps of dogmatic utterance.

Bernard Mehl

The concept of human ability, since Cattell's (1890) endeavour for establishing the facts and factors associated with it, has been subjected to a series of tests and evaluations. Studies of Binet and Simon (1905), Terman (1916), Vernon (1951), Guilford (1959) have objectively established that the ability of man differs from individual to individual. The accumulated research has also established that the ability of individuals is spread over a continuum from the feeble-minded on the one extreme to the genius or the gifted on the other end. The gifted and the geniuses are considered to be the cream of human species. They are the people who venture to explore new dimensions related to nature and cosmos. It is rightly stated that there are just 20 percent people who contribute through their superior ability, in different walks of life and thus provide facilities for the remaining 80 percent. It is unfortunate that these gifted children and geniuses are sometimes lost in the midst of crowds due to ignorance of parents, planners and policy makers. Mostly such lapses happen in the developing countries where the state is yet to gear up itself to the overall promotion of the gifted children. Developed countries like America, England and France have successfully augmented their efforts to tap educational, social and scientific resources for the proper training, placement and adequate occupational nurturance of such gifted children and geniuses.

Various theories have been devised and established which help in understanding the nature of giftedness or genius. Pathological theories have linked genius with insanity, racial degeneracy and even feeble-mindedness (Lombroso, 1895; Witty and Lehman, 1929, 1930; Kretschmer, 1931; Lang-Eichbaum, 1928, 1932, 1951). Lombroso (1895) attributed to the genius certain physical stigma short stature, rickets, pallor, emaciation, stammering, left handedness and delayed development, Kretschmer (1931), states that for true genius exceptional ability is not enough. If we take the psychopathic factor, the ferment of demonic unrest and psychic tension, away from the contribution of genius nothing but an ordinary gifted man would remain. Large-Eichbaum (1928, 32, 51), has explained associations of insanity and genius in a three fold model. First the pathological condition is said to increase the strength of the individual's emotions and his responsiveness to minute stimuli and to decrease his self control- all of which "normal" persons do not have. Secondly, those suffering from these conditions feel unhappiness and inferiority, which motivate them more strongly. Thirdly the tendency to a richer fantasy, associated with some of these disorders may be conducive to creativity of expression.

The evidence cited in support of the pathological views of genius consists of selected cases. Therefore, can not be generalized. Secondly, many geniuses may become maladjusted in a culture based on average man, his needs and aspirations. Maladjustment may become an indirect result rather than a cause or an essential component of genius. Thirdly a person, with high ability, may be sensitive to injustice and thus subjected to more emotional wear and tear. Such people are considered pathological by their fellow friends and society till their success is demonstrated and the benefits of their contribution become tangible.

Psychoanalytic conception of genius emphasizes motivational rather than intellectual characteristics (Dooley, 1916; Freud, 1925; Herzberg, 1929; Hitschmann, 1956). Wexberg (1929) advocates that genius does not differ in ability from the ordinary man but differs only what he does with his ability under strong motivational urges. Hitschman (1956) and Wexberg (1929) are of the opinion that in creative production of genius sublimation, compensation and unconscious processes are the basic sources.

The psychoanalytic viewpoint of genius does not hold good for all gifted endeavours. Strong emotional urges are not the sole means for a person to exhibit giftedness. Rossman (1931) has made an inquiry of 710 active and successful American inventors. For this group of inventors the invention was not a spectacular event but the inquiry covered both the characteristics of inventors and the nature of inventive proce s. Besides, the creative experience was on the whole very methodical, systematic, and a matter of fast process.

The view that genius inherits a qualitative superiority holds that "it" is a distinct type differentiating from the other species in the kind of ability it possesses (Hirsch, 1931). According to Hirish there are three dimensions of intelligence one "perceptual and cognitive" and it is shared by the lower animals: the second "conceptual" and is common to all mankind and third "creative intelligence" specific only to the genius. The qualitative distinction appeals to the lc gic, in the sense, that the gifted differs from the rest of mankind in his achievements, so greatly that he seems to belong to another species.

The doctrine that the gifted and the geniuses involved a qualitative superiority regards genius as the upper extreme of a continuum of ability (Galton 1826; Binnet, 1905; Terman 1917, 1926; Hollingworth 1926, 1942). According to these researchers "special gifts" are attributed in a lesser degree to all mankind. Genius is identified in concrete measurable behaviuour rather than in terms of unknown entities. After the quantification of intelligence was done through intelligence tests, giftedness emerged as an area of priority research. With the result, concern was shown towards the gifted children. And a number of studies were conducted on giftedness. The latest studies in the field are of (Chan, D. W. 2004; Adam-Byers, et al 2004; Bouchet and Falk, 2001; Swaitek, 2001; Mendex, 2000; Reis & McCoah, 2000; Ford, 1996; Moon, 1996; Sternberg, et al 1996; Scott, et al 1996; Parker 1996; Baum et al. 1996; Moon 1995; Mills and Tissot 1995; Baker 1995; Baum et al 1995; Oram, et al. 1995; Horn, 1994; Borland & Wright, 1994; Pyryt and Mendaglio, 1994; Rost & Czeschlik, 1994; Maitra 1993; Callahan and Caldwell, 1993; Hunsaer and Callahan 1993; Sayler and Brookshire, 1993; Cotangelo, et al. 1993; Barnett & Durden, 1993; Purcell, 1993; Feldman, 1993; McCall, et al. 1992; Cho, 1991; Gallagher, 1991; Crammer, 1991; Hickson, 1991; Rais and Benzulli, 1991; Treffinger, 1991; Urban, 1991; Vantassel-Baska, 1991; Venguen, et al, 1991; Vesp; and Yewchuj, 1991; Keer, et al, 1988; Gallagher, 1988; Kandu, 1988; Kumar, 1988; Parthasarthy, 1988; Raina, 1988, 1988a; Renzulli, 1988; Ediger, 1987; Ganambal, 1987; Khan, 1987, Mehdi, 1987; Feldman, 1984; Miyan, 1984; Karnes et al,, 1983; Lajoie and Shore, 1981, Lehman and Erdwins, 1981; Pandey, 1980; Vashishtha, 1980 and Witemore, 1980). But only a few studies (discussed in the review of related literature) have been conducted on gifted Achievers and Underachievers. Neglecting this area of research may imply loosing our talent that can help us in the development of the nation in every walk of life.

It has been established that high scholastic performance goes with high intelligence (Kour, 1992; Sen Barat, 1992; Garg, 1992; Devi, 1990, Thilagavathi, 1990; Chadha and Chandna, 1992; Shah, 1990; Singh, 1987; Misra, 1986; Mehrotra, 1986; Mehna, 1986; Kumar, 1986; Deshpande, 1986; Das, 1986; Maitra, 1985; Chhikara, 1985; Sween, 1984; Singh, 1984; Rajput, 1984; Patel et al, 1984; Singh, 1983; Singh, 1984; Rajput, 1984; Patel et al, 1984; Singh, 1983; Girija 1980; Kohli, 1975; Pandey and Singh, 1970; Cohlar, 1941; Freeman, 1942 and Chauncey, 1929). John (1930) quotes 189 studies, Stephens (1960) cites 111 investigation and Rao (1963) refers 835 studies in which empirically discovered relationship between intelligence and scholastic achievements has been reported to be ranging from 0.10 to 0.91. It becomes clear that there is not a complete agreement among the researchers on this point. The fact becomes obvious that some non-cognitive factors intervene and disagreement results. Keeping in view the inference drawn in the light of these studies, psychologists and educationists addressed themselves to the study of factors which go with better achievement or on the other hand the factors which interfere with better scholastic performance.

As for the nature of individual difference no two persons can have an identical type of cognitive and scholastic aptitude even though they might have been brought up under similar family, socio-economic and teaching learning conditions. Not only that, even if two persons possessing almost same level of intelligence may not earn similar scholastic achievement, one may be among the overachievers and the other among Underachievers. With the result underachievement becomes a priority issue for researchers to ponder over. A host of studies have been conducted on Underachievers and overAchievers, Achievers and non-Achievers. Authors like Cattell (1961, 1965), Taylor (1964), Entwistle and Conigham (1968), Oakland (1969), Entiwistle and Entiwistle (1970), Sinha (1970), Barton, et al (1972), Menon (1972), Agarwal, (1975), Chuman (1976), Iyer (1977), Patel and Joshi (1977), Koul (1978), Mohan and Khera (1978), D'Lima (1979), Joseph (1979), Nagpal (1979), Pacholi (1980), Saun (1980), Somasundaran (1980), Sharma (1981), Singh (1983), Singh (1986), Sintakay (1986), Kapoor (1987), Puri (1987), Sahoo (1987), Haq (1988), Deb and Grewal (1990) Kotesware (1991), Rejyoguru (1991), Mathur (1992), Ford (1996), Reis & McCoah (2000) and many others have banked upon non-intellectual factors as predicators of academic achievement and over and underachievement. Keeping in view a number of studies addressed to the factors associated with under and over achievement, it is felt that gifted children must be properly taken care of before their giftedness is executed for scholastic purposes. There are chances that they may continue with their inadequacies without realizing their gifted potential. Therefore, these factors of gifted under-achievement merit an intensive study and investigation.

India is a populous country of all shades and persuasions, it lacks specialists in various developmental programmes because of inadequate attention towards the gifted. As intelligence is normally distributed, majority of gifted children remain uncared. With the result, a great chunk of wouldbe technocrats, scientists and the academicians either do not attend school at all or attend school but prove to be Underachievers, laggers and failures. Thus the country loses brilliant minds who could lead the nation in the technological and industrial fields. The need of the hour is to discover every gifted child and expose him to the field for which he is talented and ensure that he receives all the education from which he can benefit himself in particular and society in general. Otherwise gifted children, when not provided with proper nourishment and direction for their talent, contribute to the increasing number of Underachievers in the school. Obviously, they themselves also face problems in their adjustment.

Miyan (1988), observes that for self reliance in various fields – agriculture, industry, engineering, telecommunication, defence, India needs highly capable personnel who are not only able to maintain but evolve alternate strategies with given resources and replace outdated technology with a more efficient one. Thus there is an increasing demand of highly talented citizens to assume complex roles in the society. The survival of this planet depends on how successfully the potential of the gifted and talented children is realized and integrated (Lyon, 1976). In a national seminar on gifted children in the year 1984, Tripathy and Misra state in their article under the subheading “Research Gaps and Priorities”. “In the context of tests, identification and characteristics all the studies are concerned with the sample from Urban and semi-urban areas, without considering the tribal and rural areas”. The need and importance for the placement of the gifted has been underlined by various commissions. The Radha Krishnan Commission (1948-49) has made a strong plea for making special provisions for the education of the gifted and the talented, who would take leadership positions in various walks of life in independent India. In fact the gifted and the talented are the ‘seed people, concept changers, and pulse-takers’ of society. In the same Vein Chaudhari (1988) states that the survival of the democracy is contingent upon its capability to educate the superior or promising citizens. In spite of the tall claims of Indian Education

Commission (1964-66), "Need of the search and development of talent", underachievement of the gifted remains totally uncared for and needs the attention of educationists, psychologists and scholars. On the recommendations of New Education Policy (1986) a network of Navodaya Vidyalaya schools for the gifted in the whole country has been established. As giftedness has become a national priority area, the investigator felt concerned about gifted Underachievers of rural Kashmir. Despite, the increasing interest in education of the gifted stimulated by the growing need to meet the scientific and technological changes of the space era, very little attention has been directed to the gifted Underachievers (Waddington and O' Brien, 1979; Freeman, 1979; Davis and Rimm, 1985; Gallegher, 1985; Khan, 1987). The reasons for this neglect lie in the difficulties encountered by the concerned parents and teachers in recognizing the ability of the young children. In India parents, in general, are unconcerned about their children due to ignorance. They hardly realize the importance of their child and his talent. They want him to be their helping hand in the routine chores.

Giftedness is not manifested in normal convergent school behviour; it is difficult for the teachers to recongize this ability (Khan, 1987). Therefore, under these conditions the gifted underachiever is the greatest sufferer. Keeping this consideration in mind the present piece of research intends to explore the characteristics which go with gifted Underachievers.

A host of characteristics have been associated with achievement and underachievement. Educational research has shown that the achievement of a pupil is related to the group and class he/she belongs to and as such attempts have been made to estimate the socio-economic status of an individual and relate it to his scholastic attainment. Garrison (1932) found SES has a great impact on scholastic achievement than intellectual ability. Menon (1972) found over-achievement and underachievement to be influenced by SES. Anastasi (1960), Mohan and Khera (1978) have found that SES has a positive influence upon scholastic attainment. Khanna (1980) established a significant and positive relationship between SES and academic achievement. Sarkar (1983), established that SES of high and low Achievers differs significantly. Jagannaddan (1985), has found a significant effect of home environment on academic achievement. In view of the above findings, there seems to be a significant difference between the SES of gifted Achievers and Underachievers.

In the achievement related areas, need for achievement (N.Ach), has been found to be a significant variable, which contributes to the better performance of a person. Deshpande (1984), Sween (1984), Rai (1980), Shivappa (1980), Pathak (1974), Sinha (1970), Mehta (1967, 69), Atkinson (1958), McClelland et al. (1953), have found significant correlation between scholastic performance and Need achievement (N Ach.) as a personality variable has been related with the academic performance and the studies have shown that the presence or absence of such motivation affects the results in a decisive manner but how does this factor relate itself to the question of gifted underachievement and achievement, is yet to be established. The present investigator therefore, besides other factors, addressed himself to this aspect of the problem as well.

Mahamahopadyay and Byti (1986), have found that high Achievers are socially welladjusted, more mature, active, energetic, confident, happy and alert. Mohan and Virdi (1985) report that persistence is a significant factor in high achievement. Jerome (1984), has found that the underachiever is deficient in attention and concentration. Natesan and Devi (1987) have provided that high and low Achievers differ on the traits of emotional stability, boldness and self assurance. Sharma (1972) has found that overAchievers are better adjusted than Underachievers on all areas of adjustment – school, home, social, religious and miscellaneous. Dhaliwali (1971), has revealed that emotional instability and happy-go-lucky temperament are associated with academic underachievement, whereas, emotional stability, poor social adjustment correspond to over-achievement. Mohan and Khera (1978) have established that Underachievers are predominantly high on the factors of super-ego, strength and premier. Over Achievers were found to show significant difference from Underachievers on the factors of absent mindedness and guilt proneness. Naylor (1972), has rightly stated that it is conceivable that other personality characteristics (besides intelligence) have a systematic effect on performance. Personality adjustment, which affects performance, is one of the most important characteristics of underachievement. It is obvious from the research studies cited above that high and low Achievers, under/over Achievers differ significantly so far as their personality characteristics are concerned. Gifted Achievers and Underachievers may also decidedly differentiate in their personality factors, hence it merits investigation.

Statement of the Problem

The review of literature highlights that a number of studies have been conducted on Achievers and overachievers, Achievers and Underachievers and the gifted in general in relation to neuroticism, self concept, level of aspiration, adjustment, personality and need achievement. But hardly any study has been completed on gifted Achievers and Underachievers with respect to personality factors, socioeconomic status and Need Achievement, especially on a sample from rural background. The rural children are almost cut-off from the modern society and live a life of backwardness. Under this backdrop the present study addressed itself to an understanding of personality profiles, Need Achievement and Socio-economic status of gifted Achievers and Underachievers in rural Kashmir. The problem proposed for the study was formulated as :-

> "*Gifted Achievers and Underachievers - Their Personality Profiles, Need Achievement and Socio-economic Status.*"

Need and Importance of the Study

It would be inforced that space age has generated an interest in the psychological and education factors contributing to the underachievement of the gifted students. India is already facing the highest illiteracy rate, wastage and stagnation and above all brain drain. Therefore, it becomes more pertinent to care for the talented. Due to underachievement, gifted talent gets lost among the millions. Even for that matter they become social deviants or continue as laggers.

As high achievement goes with high intelligence is an established fact, the author is baffled by the fact that about 50% bright subjects, in rural Kashmir are Underachievers (Khan, 1987), whereas in England the corresponding position is 25% (Whitemore, 1980).

Children are not born Underachievers, their school behaviour is acquired (Davis and Rim, 1985), and fortunately, as the authors experience has shown that teachers can be very effective in helping underachieving children if and only if they are aware about certain characteristic features of the gifted Underachievers. But despite some studies conducted in this field, we do not have a clear profile of personality traits and social class background, that would characterize gifted Underachievers and Achievers.

Exploring the personality dispositions, Needs Achievement and Socio-economic status of both gifted Achievers and Underachievers can serve an excellent purpose in helping the concerned – parents, teachers and counsellors for suitably identifying and rehabilitating them.

Objectives

The study was undertaken with the following objectives in view:-

01. To identify gifted subjects.
02. To identify the gifted Achievers and under-Achievers.
03. To find out the personality factors of gifted Achievers and Underachievers.
04. To find the relative position of gifted Achievers and Underachievers on n.Ach.
05. To study the SES of gifted Achievers and Underachievers.
06. To find out the factors which go together with gifted Achievers and Underachievers.

Hypotheses

Keeping in view the objectives of the present study, the following hypotheses were set up for testing:-

01. Gifted Achievers and Underachievers differ significantly so far as their personality factors are concerned.
02. In comparison to gifted Underachievers, gifted Achievers possess significantly high Need Achievement.
03. The SES of gifted Achievers is significantly better than gifted Underachievers.

04. The factor pattern associated with gifted Achievers is decidedly different from gifted Underachievers.

Operational Definitions of Variables

The Gifted:

During all the periods of history, superior ability of people has been honoured in refined cultures. As early as 2200 B.C., the Chinese had developed an elaborate system of competitive examination to select outstanding persons for Governmental positions (Dubois, 1970). The Turks and the Greeks also followed the same path. But at the end of the nineteenth century and the beginning of 20th century scholars expressed discontentment with the haphazard selection of "the gifted" through arbitrary standards and sought to define 'giftedness' in a more precise, systematic and empirical way. However, despite, the plethora of research studies conducted on the gifted, no universally accepted definition of giftedness has emerged. Some well known definitions of giftedness are as under:-

> "*The top one percent level in general intellectual ability, as measured by the standard – Binet Intelligence Scale or a comparable instrument.*"
>
> (Terman, et al., 1926, p. 43).

> "*We consider any child gifted whose performance, in a potentially valuable line of human activity, is consistently remarkable*".
>
> (Witty, 1958, p. 62).

> "*a talented or gifted child is one who shows consistently remarkable performance in any worthwhile line of endeavour. Thus, we shall include not only the intellectual gifted but also those who show promise in music, the*

graphic arts, creative writing, dramatics, mechanical skills and social leadership."

(57th Year Book, 1958, p. 19).

The definition of gifted children set forth by the United States Office of Education, has grown in popularity and is widely used throughout the States. The definition reads as under:-

"Gifted and talented children are those, identified by professionally qualified persons, who by virtue of outstanding abilities are capable of high performance. These are children who require differentiated educational programmes and/or services beyond those normally provided by the regular school programmes in order to realize their contribution to self and society. Children capable of high performance include those with demonstrated achievement and/or potential in any of the following areas, singly or in combination:

1. *General Intellectual Ability*
2. *Special Academic aptitude*
3. *Creative or productive thinking*
4. *Leadership ability*
5. *Visual and Performing Arts*
6. *Psychomotor ability."*

(Marland, 1972, p. 2).

"Giftedness is composed of three basic characteristics; above average general ability, high level of task commitment, and high level of creativity. Gifted and talented children are those possessing or capable of developing this composite set of traits and

applying them to any potentially valuable areas of human performance.".

(Renzulli and Delisle, 1982, p. 727).

High intellectual potential is a thread that goes through all the definitions of gifted persons. Therefore, "High I.Q." has been fixed as the criteria for "giftedness" in the present study. Operationally the term "gifted" has been defined as under:-

> "*Subjects whose intelligence scores on a mental measurement test (Ravan's APM) fall above 80th percentile, will be considered as gifted.*".

The criterion model is in line with (Maitra, 1991; Lidhoo and Khan, 1990 and Bhatnagar, 1976).

Gifted Achievers:

McClelland (1989) used Achievement/I.Q. discrepancy scores, having measured achievement and I.Q. by standardized tests, to identify gifted Achievers and gifted Underachievers. Both groups had I.Q. scores in the gifted range, but the gifted Achievers scored at least one and one half standard deviation above the mean discrepancy score, whereas gifted Underachievers scored at least one and one half standard deviation below the same mean score.

(Cit. In, Wilgosh, 1991, p.83).

The operational definition of Gifted Achievers in the present study is as under:-

> "*Gifted subjects whose mean achievement scores of the previous two annual examination results lie minus 10 percentile or above, their intelligence percentile scores will be considered gifted Achievers.*"

In order to qualify the above-mentioned definition, it is desirable to mention that academic achievement scores of two annual examinations (8th and 9th) for 10th class students and (7th and 8th) for 9th class students were averaged and converted into percentages in order to serve as an index of academic achievement of each sample subject. This was done in order to minimize the possibility of any intervening effect. The percentiles were calculated for both achievement and intelligence scores.

Gifted Underachievers

> "*The Underachievers with special ability are those whose performance, as judged either by grades or achievement test scores, is significantly below his high measured or demonstrated aptitude or potential for academic achievement.*"
>
> (Shaw, 1964, p. 325).

Most of the researchers define Underachievers by the large gap between the Underachievers' school performance and potential. However, since it is not possible to assess this potential accurately, investigators usually define on the basis of I.Q. scores, while achievement is assessed on the concerned subject (Raph et al, 1966). In the present study the same line of action has been followed for the identification of gifted Underachievers. Operationally Gifted Underachievers in the present study are defined as under:-

> "*Gifted subjects whose mean achievement scores of previous two annual examination results lie 10 percentiles or below, their intelligence percentile scores, will be considered gifted Underachievers*".

The criterion model for defining gifted Achievers and Underachievers is in line with (Gowan, 1960; Mohan and Nehru, 1972; Mohan and Khera, 1978).

Personality

Popular meaning of the personality falls under one of the two headlines. The first equates the term with social skill. An individuals personality is assessed by the effectiveness with which he or she is able to elicit positive reactions from a variety of persons under different circumstances. The second considers the personality of the individual to consist of the impression he or she creates on others e.g. submissive or aggressive personality. There is an element of evaluation in both the usages. Personalities as such are good or bad. Allport (1937) speaks of biophysical and bio-social definitions of personality. Bio-social definition equates personality with the "Social stimulus value" of the individual measured in terms of the reaction of other individuals to the subject. It is the other person who speaks abut one's personality, Biophysical definition roots personality in the personal characteristics and qualities of the subject. According to biophysical concept, personality has an organic as well as perceived side and may be linked with the specific qualities of the individual susceptible to objective measurement and description. Allport (1961) treats personality as a unit "out there" possessing internal structure in its own right. Some definitions lay stress on unique quality (Stagner, 1961; Allport, 1961) others in terms of fixed stages (Freud, 1933; Erikson, 1963; Piaget and Inhelder, 1969) and still others see personality in terms of organisation of traits (Eysench, 1953; Cattell, 1970).

Taking into account the confusion and difficulty regarding the meaning and nature of personality, Hall and Lindzey (1989) have presented a general definition of personality, which has been adopted in the present study.

> *"Personality consists concretely of a set of scores of descriptive terms that describe the*

individual being studied in the terms of the variables or dimensions that occupy a central position within the particular theory utilized."

(Hall & Lindzey, p. 09).

Personality Profiles:

"*Personality profiles will refer to the significantly clustering factors in terms of Cattell's High School Personality Questionnaire (HSPQ).*"

Need Achievement (N.Ach.)

Murry (1938) is the first man who has coined the term Need Achievement. His taxonomy of human needs distinguished and defined 28 needs, each designated by abbreviation such as n Aff (affiliation need), n Dom (Dominace need) ..... N. Ach (Achievement need). He defined need Achievement as –

"*.... The desire or tendency to do things as rapidly and/or as well as possible.*"

Mukjerjee purports to measure only one need through Incomplete Sentence Blank (ISB). That is need for achievement. He has defined need achievement as follows –

"*behaviour which shows effort to do one's best or excel others.*"

(Mukjerjee, 1968, p. 01).

Mukherjee's definition has been considered as an operational definition for the present study.

Socio-economic Status:

Socio economic status is an important variable in the planning of developmental programme and in researches in the field of Sociology, Education, Psychology, Community Development. A plethora of research studies have been conducted where it has been shown that socio-economic status influences social participation, academic achievement, leadership styles, motivation, vocational performances, need achievement, study habits, sociometric status etc. Socio-economic status has been defined differently by different authors (Chapin, 1928l Lewis and Dhillon, 1955; Kuppuswamy 1959; Freeman, 1961; Verma, 1962; Pareek and Trivedi, 1964; Madhosh and Rafiqui, 1990). There is a thread that goes along almost all the definitions, i.e. three variables: education, occupation and income loom large. Taking the definitions of all the authors into account, socioeconomic status has been operationally defined in the present study as under:-

> "*Status of parents/guardians, which is spread over caste, occupation, education, income, house, farm possession, social participation, farm power and animal possession, material position of the family and family type.*"

The focus:

01. The sample for the present study comprises of 9th and 10th class students on the basis that this is the stage in their life when childish manners have gone and they become mature to take decisions for themselves.

02. The study was confined to the rural areas of Kashmir.

03. The study was confined to all the schools of two tehsils of Kashmir valley only.

04. Age and sex was controlled in order to avoid any intervention in the results. Therefore, only boys were included in the present study.

05. Keeping time and financial constraints in view the study was confined to the variables like personality profiles, Need Achievement and Socio-economic status of Gifted Achievers and Under-Achievers.

Review of Literature

If we could first know where we are and whither we are tending, we would better judge what to do and how to do it.

Abraham Lincoln

A worthwhile study in any field of knowledge demands an adequate familiarity with the work which has been conducted in that field. It is only through the accumulation of the recorded knowledge of the past that a researcher, utilizes the previous finding in order to enunciate a sound research design. He locates comparative data that is useful in the interpretation of results, develops an insight to formulate appropriate hypothesis, explains ideas in a lucid manner, enriches his personal scholarship and prevents repetition of research.

Justification for any new scientific or descriptive research can not be there unless gaps in the existing knowledge are located or controversy if any is established on any unresolved issue. In order to save the present study from hanging loosely in the air, a detailed survey of the related literature viz. evaluated reports of relevant researches conducted in India and abroad, published articles in the professional journals, research abstracts, pertinent pages of allied manuscripts and relevant portions of encyclopaedias was made. The appropriate literature has been placed under four headings as follows:

I. Gifted Achievers and Underachievers- their personality;

II. Gifted Achievers and Underachievers-their need achievement;

III. Gifted Achievers and Underachievers - their socioeconomic status;

IV. Gifted Achievers and Underachievers-their personality and need achievement; personality and socioeconomic status; need achievement and socio-economic status; personality need achievement and socio-economic status.

I. Gifted Achievers and under-Achievers -- their personality

Morgan, H.H. (1952) *A psychometric comparison of Achieving and non-achieving college students of High ability.*

Morgan compared a group of college Achievers with under-Achievers of high ability (top 10%). The major difference found between the two groups on the tests of personality and interest was that non-Achievers possessed psychopathic personality. On the other hand high Achievers scored higher in the areas of dominance and self confidence, social responsibility, motivation to achieve and, awareness and concern for others. A marked difference in the interest patterns was also found. Achievers were more interested in social service and welfare occupations while non-Achievers had interest patterns which resembled those of persons in business or sales occupations.

Gowan, J.C. (1957) *Dynamics of the underachievement of Gifted students.*

Gown has summarized some of the studies conducted on under-achieving gifted children, by some of the investigators and has concluded that the factors related to underachievement are, week ego controls; neurotic tendencies; lack of dominance; persuasiveness; and self-confidence; apathetic and withdrawing view of life; lack of maturity and irresponsibility; disinterest in other people; withdrawal and self sufficiency; poor use of time and money; authoritarianism in the home; no goals or impossible demands of parents; lack of clearness and definiteness of academic and occupational choice; dominant, autocratic or *laisez-faire* parents.

Durr, W.K. and Collier (1960).

Recent Research on the gifted consists of comparisons of gifted Underachievers with Achievers. One of the most thorough studies reported in the survey was conducted on gifted children in grades four, five and six. forty seven high Achievers gifted and thirty four gifted low Achievers were compared on personality and mental health. The results revealed significant difference between the groups on personal adjustment. Low achieving students indicated withdrawing tendencies and to lack of self reliance, a sense of personal worth, a sense of personal freedom and a feeling of belongingness. Mental health analysis revealed that low achieving gifted children were more likely to show behavioural immaturity, emotional instability feeling of inadequacy than were high achieving gifted children. High Achievers saw themselves as freer to make choices and to communicate with their parents than did low-Achievers. The high Achievers had greater feeling of individual worth, greater ability to persist in the face of difficulties, and greater ability to cope with their own emotional disturbances.

Davids, A (1966). *Psychological characteristics of high school male and female potential scientists in comparison with academic Underachievers.*

Davids compared achieving and non achieving high I.Q. gifted students of high school age and found that achieving boys were higher on dominance, endurance, order and introspection, and that low achieving boys were higher on need for nurturing and hetro-sexuality. Both the achieving boys and girls were higher on self control than the low-achieving subjects. It was also found that male and female high achieving were higher than that of low Achievers on self assurance, socialization and maturity.

Bachtold, L.M. (1969) *Personality differences among high ability Underachievers.*

Bachtold compared different groups of seven through nine grade underachieving gifted students to one another and high achieving gifted students. Girls who scored low on standard achievement tests but made good grades were similar to girls who did well on both. Girls who had good achievement test scores but obtained low grades were less credulous, confident, and self controlled but more evitable than the other female groups. Boys who had high grades but were weak on standardised tests were more serious than other male group. Boys who were showing under-achievement on both tests and grades were less sensitive than the boys who were successful on both or in only one area. High ability, high achieving males were emotionally stable, serious and sensitive. High ability, high achieving female were characterised by credulity, self-confidence and self-control.

Menon, S.K. (1972). *A comparative study of personality characteristics of overAchievers and Underachievers of high ability.*

The study was conducted to find out the relationship between underachievement and certain personality characteristic such as social activity, extroversion/ introversion, tolerance, maladjustment and masculinity; certain motivational traits like academic interests, general ambition, persistence and endurance; certain areas of interest like outdoor, aesthetic, scientific, mechanical, persuasive, clerical and social service. Influence of social and demographic factors on the problem of underachievement was also ascertained. The main findings of the study were: Over-achieving group of superior boys and girls were less extrovert and less maladjusted than Underachievers and showed greater academic interest and endurance; demographic factors and socio-economic status markedly influenced over and underachievement. Higher occupational and educational level of father, educational level of mother, family income and parental attention were related to high achievement, but the extent of relationship was not similar for boys and girls. Job aspiration, educational aspiration and general ambition were strongly associated with high achievement particularly in case of girls.

Sontaky, G. R. (1975). *An experimental study of Bright Under-achieving boys.*

The study was conducted to identify factors responsible for effecting the achievement of bright students. Fifty bright under-achieving and achieving male students were selected from 11-16 year old students at five boys middle schools on the basis of verbal intelligence, Teacher ratings and academic achievement. The subjects were administered problems and study habit inventories, self concept blank and an interview was conducted with subjects, parents and teachers. The results made it obvious that emotional problems of Underachievers were greater than those of overAchievers; Underachievers possessed poor health in general. The study habits of overAchievers were better than those of Underachievers. Over-Achievers had positive self-concept and were co-operative and sociable.

Kulshrestha, L. (1981). *A study of certain factors related to differential patterns of achievement among bright students.*

The major objectives of the investigation were to study the relationship between the achievement and personality characteristics of bright students; to find out how parental attitude, family background and basic skills influenced academic achievement of bright students; to find out the effect of vocational interest on the achievement of bright students. The sample comprised 276 students screened out of 1,050 first year science and mathematics students, on the basis of general mental ability test of Joshi. The main findings of the study were: the bright underachievers in mathematics were more warm hearted than normal Achievers and bright normal Achievers in English were more conscientious than bright Underachievers; the bright normal and Underachievers in science and mathematics differed in their attitude to parents whereas the common students did not; the bright normal Achievers in English possessed significantly higher basic skills in English than bright Underachievers in English, Underachievement was related, to some extent, with economic conditions at home but not with personal health of the students; Underachievers lived in more noisy houses; the vocational interest in agricultural, persuasive, social and household areas had a changing role in scholastic achievement, less interest in these areas helped in achieving high. Whereas greater interest was detrimental to achievement; the bright

Underachievers showed greater vocational interests in artistic and agricultural areas than other students. Bright Underachievers in mathematics were more interested in vocations related to household areas than normal Achievers.

Sternberg, R.J. (1986) *Intelligence applied; understanding and increasing your intellectual skills.*

Some of the important personality characteristics which hinder underachiever's progress are:

a) Lack of motivation
b) Lack of impulsive control
c) Lack of persistence/preseration or perservence
d) Capitalizing on the wrong abilities
e) Inability or difficulty in translating thought into action
f) Lack of product orientation
g) Task completion problems
h) Failure to initiate
i) Procastination
j) Misattribution of blame
k) Excessive self-pity-feeling sorry for one-self
l) Wallowing in personal difficulties
m) Distractibility and lack of attention
n) Spreading one-self too thick or too thin
o) Inability to delay gratification
p) Inability or unwillingness to see the forest from the trees
q) Lack of balance between critical analytic thinking and creative synthetic thinking

r) Too little or too much self-confidence.

Swensson, O. K. (1986). *Classroom Behaviours of Male Academically Gifted Underachievers, Academically gifted Achievers and Average Students: A comparative study.*

The goal of this study was to identify overt attentional and interactional behaviours directly related to underachievement by observing the underachiever within the regular classroom and then comparing this behaviour to that of the academically gifted achiever and the average learner. The behaviours targeted for study those most consistently associated with school achievement; attentional behaviour and interactions which involve a higher level of student attention (e.g. volunteering, pupil initial work contacts). The results indicate that no significant differences were found between the subject types on any of the eight behavioral categories rated. Results of the survey of teacher perceptions of classroom behaviour differed from those of the observational study. Significant differences were perceived by teachers between the academically gifted underachiever with respect to hostility, distractibility, independence, task orientation and consideration. There was no significant variation in the teachers perceptions of the underachiever and the average student.

Thomson, A. K. (1986) *Depression and underachievement in the Gifted Male Adolescents.*

The relationship between depression and underachievement in a gifted male high school population was assessed using the total score and ten subscales of Berndt's Multiple Depression Inventory (MD) as predictor variables in a multiple discriminant analysis. Achievers and Underachievers group defined by GPA constituted the criterion variable.

In the initial study using data from 63 of those students whose grades were at the extremes of the GPA continuum, the depression syndrome as defined by MDI did not significantly discriminate between Achievers and Underachievers, However one variable, cognitive difficulty, formed a factor which did discriminate between the two criterion group. Cognitive difficulty takes the form of jumbled thoughts, a lack of clarity and precision in thinking, and indecisiveness.

Data from the 44 students in the middle of GPA continuum permitted several additional analysis. In an analysis having low and high underachiever groups and low and high achiever groups, five depression components entered the analysis to form a function separating the underachiever group from achiever group. The components were pessimism, cognitive difficulty, energy level (fatigue), learnal and instrumental helplessness. The resulting significant function primarily reflects a pessimistic view of the future along with subjective sense of cognitive dysfunction. This function accounted for 16% of the variance in group membership.

Other findings pointed out a heterogeneity in reporting symptoms within the underachieving group. The low Underachievers (GPA of 2.75 or below) reported fewer symptoms on some subscales than the high Underachievers (GPA of 2.75 to 2.99). Upper under Achievers reported the most of symptoms and the Achievers report the fewest symptoms.

Mufson, L. et al. (1989). *Factors Associated with Underachievement in seventh Grade children.*

Twenty-three seventh grade students were studied to identify emotional, social, or cognitive variable that might contribute to lower than predicated scholastic performance of bright subjects. All sample subjects in this study received high scores on the California Achievement test (percentile score of 90-100). The subjects who were designated as Achievers attained all A's as final grade for the previous years (6th grade) whereas those designated as Underachievers received grade B to C range. The two groups of subjects were evaluated and compared through student, parent and teacher interviews and questionnaires. The results of this study revealed that Underachievers were less self-confident, less socially and emotionally mature, less able to focus on one concern at a time, less accurate in their perceptions about themselves and their work, and less hardworking. Underachievers had less ability to communicate with their parents and believed that their parents were less interested in their school work. Compared with the Achievers, Underachievers believed that their parents were less strict.

II. Gifted Achievers and Underachievers - their need achievement

Pirece, J.V. (1959). *The Educational Motivational pattern of Superior Students who do and do not Achieve in High School.*

On the characteristics of desire to achieve, it was found that 10th and 12th graders-both boys and girls valued achievement more highly than did low achieving students, with the exception of the 12th grade boys. The high achieving boys and girls valued the concepts of school, work and imagination more than did their low achieving students and also rated the concepts of self, student and competition higher. High achieving students were more active in school-related activities and leadership activities. In the general area of emotional adjustment, the high Achievers were also better adjusted as measured by tests of personality.

Pirece, J. V. and Bowman, P. U. (1960). *Motivation pattern of superior high school students- The Gifted students.*

The study was conducted on high intelligent subjects of 10th and 12th class. The subjects were top thirty percent scorers in intellectual ability. The subjects were divided into high and low achieving subjects on the basis of achievement intelligence discrepancy. The high Achievers showed a higher achievement motivation than the low achieving subjects. High Achievers had greater expectancy for academic success than the low Achievers.

Zilli, M. J. (1971). *Reasons why Gifted Adolescent Underachieves and some of the Implications of Guidance and councelling to this problem.*

Zilli has reviewed the literature and summarized her finding in following major causes of under-achievement: a) inadequate motivation; b) social pressure or maladjustment; c) Specifically inadequate curriculum content and poor teaching; d) a school atmosphere low in intellectual stimulation and challenge, or teacher emphasis on conformity; e) personality characteristics and unsuitable home climate.

Chaudhari, V. P. (1975). *Factors contributing to Academic Under-achievement.*

The objective of the study was to make a critical study of the factors contributing to academic under-achievement. In order to obtain a sample of 300 bright Underachievers bright Achievers and dull Achievers a large group of 3,500 students was taken. The major findings of the study were: Achievement motivation of bright Achievers was higher than that of bright Underachievers; dull Achievers had low achievement motivation than bright under-Achievers. Difference in the mean score of N-achievement of two groups was sharper in the case of boys than in girls. Achievers who had high level of achievement motivation had minimum anxiety. Girls in comparison with boys of respective groups had higher achievement motivation. The study habits of Achievers differed significantly on Sinha's Anxiety scale; Underachievers differed from Achievers at 0.05 level and from dull Achievers at 0.01 level. Bright Achievers normally came from families where parents had higher level of education and had more income than the parents of dull children. The mothers of bright Achievers had higher level of education than the mothers of Underachievers. Bright achieving female candidates had better general adjustment.

Fleming, W. W. M. (1985). *Attribution styles of Gifted High and low achieving Adolescents.*

The purpose of this study was to investigate the relationship between achievement behaviour and attributional style in gifted high school students. Specifically this research was aimed at determining: if gifted high and low achieving adolescent differed in their attributions for success and failure or helpless mastery orientation and if there were gender differences in attribution style, helpless mastery orientation. Further more, this investigation was to explore Seligman's (1975) concept of internality stability and globality in relation to attributions while expanding the literature on specific aspects of attribution theory - the learned helplessness phenomenon-by examining its relationship to the achievement behaviour in gifted adolescents.

The results of this study indicate that high and low achieving students did not differ significantly in their causal attributions for success or failure outcomes along the dimensions of internality. Both high and low achieving students attributed positive outcome to internal, stable and global causes, although the negative outcome situations were attributed on a much more situation basis on the internality, globality and stability dimensions. Additionally results indicated that high and low Achievers were not differentiated on helpless mastery orientation in their response to negative outcomes in school achievement situations. Both groups tended to be more helpless than mastery oriented. Both gifted boys and girls attributed positive outcome situations to internal causes, whereas attributions to negative outcome situations are made contingent on the situation.

Francoys, G.(1985). *Giftedness and Talent: re-examining a re-examination of the definitions.*

Several common definitions of the term giftedness and Talent, with particular emphasis on the models proposed by J. S. Ranzulli (1979) and S. J. Cohan (1981) have been discussed. The critique of these two models leads to a clear definition between giftedness and Talent. The performance is associated with domains of abilities that foster and explain exceptional performance in varied fields of activities, that is, talents. Thus an individual can be gifted without necessary being talented (as in the case of Underachievers) but not the vice-versa. Several factors that can act as catalysts for the actualization of giftedness in specific talents and are discussed particularly motivation and environmental quality.

Krishna Maitra (1985). *Affective Correlates of Gifted Under-Achievers.*

The study was designed to find out the impact of the affective variables on academic achievement of pupils, who were other-wise intellectually gifted. the identification of the sample of gifted overAchievers 129 and gifted Underachievers III was done from 24 public school of Delhi, reading in VII class. The tools used for the identification of sample and collection of data were:

i. Reven's progressive Matrices (1960)
ii. Perception about the Home scale Developed
iii. Perception about the school scale by the
iv. Academic self concept scale investigator
v. N-Ach. Test (P.Mehra).

The findings of the study revealed that (a) under-achievement indicated significant correlation with the perception about `Home' for gifted Underachievers (G-U); (b) Academic under-achievement and perception about 'school' maintained significant correlation for the gifted underachievement; (c) for G-U., Academic under-achievement and academic self concept did correlate significantly; (d) There was a significant relationship between academic underachievement and achievement motivation for G-U; (e) The perception about home of the G-U correlated significantly with perception about school; (f) The perception and home of the G-U correlated significantly with their academic self concept; (g) there existed a significant correlation between the perception about school and the academic self concept of the gifted Achievers, (h) the academic self concept and achievement motivation for the G.U did not show any clear relationship. The case studies of some school Underachievers revealed that they were mostly over protected, had more than one or two siblings, mothers were housewives, had lack of intellectual encouragement at home, and irregular study habits. The perception of school was the same for G.U and gifted overAchievers. The achievement was found to be independent of SES.

Ames, C. and Archer, J. (1988). *Achievement Goals in the classroom Students learning strategies and Motivation processes.*

The study was designed to study how specific motivational processes are related to the salience of mastery and performance goals in actual classroom setting. One hundred seventy six students attending a junior high/high school for academically advanced students were randomly selected from one of their classes and responded to a questionnaire on their perceptions of the classroom goal orientation, use of effective learning strategies, task choices, attitudes, and causal attributions. Students who perceived an emphasis on mastery goals in the classroom reported using more effective strategies, preferred challenging tasks, had a more positive attitude towards the class, and had a stronger belief that success follows from ones effort. Students who perceived performance goals as salient tended to focus on their ability evaluating their ability negatively and attributing failure to lack of ability. The pattern and strength of the findings suggest that the classroom goal orientation may facilitate the maintenance of adaptive motivation patterns when master goals are salient and are adopted by students.

Baum, S. & Owen, S. V. (1988). *High Ability/Learning Disabled Students: How are they different?*

The purpose of the research was to investigate characteristics that distinguish high ability/LD students from learning disabled students with average cognitive ability and from high ability students. One hundred twelve high ability or learning disabled students in grades four, five and six participated in the study: High ability, High ability/LD and LD/average. Discriminant analysis indicated that the three groups are distinguishable: High ability/LD students show high levels of creative potential accompanied by low levels of academic success and a tendency towards disruptive behaviour. These youngsters think that school offers plenty of occasions for failure, and they often ascribe their academic failures to shyness. In contrast to high ability students, High ability/LD students experience fewer school successes and considerably more failures. Even compared with less able learning disabled students, the High ability/Learning Disabled students perceived themselves frequently as failures in school. Their feeling of academic ineptness probably increases motivation to avoid school tasks.

III. Gifted Achievers and Underachievers - their need socio-economic status

Gallagher, J. J. (1960). *Analysis of Research on Education of Gifted Children.*

Gallagher after surveying the literature concerning Underachievers among the children of superior intelligence presents a combination of events which leads to underachievement:

i. The underachieving child grows up in , or belongs to, a cultural group which does not value education, independence or individual achievement;

ii. He has poor parental relationships in which the parents, especially the father either shows limited interest in his academic matters, or try to put undue pressure on their children to succeed;

iii. Teachers ask these children to meet standards of behaviour, which are not possible for them. The children thus place the teachers in the same authority category as parents and reject them and their programme; .

iv. The school, in its attempt to deal with these nonconforming children, take strict and repressive measures which turns these children more against the school.

Curry, R. L. (1962). *The Effect of Socioeconomic Status on the Scholastic Achievement of Sixth Grade Children.*

Curry has found that socioeconomic status seems to have no effect upon the scholastic achievement of 6th grade students when the students have high intellectual ability. But social and economic factors have an effect upon language achievement in the medium intellectual ability group. Both the upper and the middle socio-economic status groups achieve greater than the lower SES group. In total achievement, the upper SES group fared better than the lower SES group. So far as the lower intellectual ability group is concerned, he points out that social and economic factors have an effect on achievement in reading, language, and total achievement. In reading, the upper SES group shows a greater amount of achievement than the middle and lower SES group. Curry suggests that as the intellectual ability decreases from high to low, the affect of social and economic conditions on scholastic achievement increases greatly.

Morrow, W.R. & Wilson, F.C (1967). *Family relations of bright high achieving and under-achieving school boys.*

The study was designed to find out the family relationship of bright high achieving and underachieving school boys. A sample of high school students of superior intelligence was carefully grouped into high and low Achievers. The family relationships of sample subjects were ascertained by a questionnaire and a few open ended questions. The results make it clear that bright high Achievers' parents reportedly engage in more sharing of activities ideas and confidence, and more approving and trusting, affectionate and encouraging with respect to achievement and are less restricted and sever. The Underachievers' parents show more over protectiveness, high pressure for achievement and disharmony in the family. Family morale foster academic achievement among bright high school boys via fostering positive attitude towards teachers, school and interest in intellectual activities.

Delisle, J. et al. (1987). *Preventing discipline Problems with Gifted Students.*

Delisle, Whitemore and Ambrose (1987) have mentioned following as reasons for underachievement:

1. A perceived lack of genuine respect from parents or teachers for each individual.
2. A competitive social climate
3. Inflexibility and rigidity
4. Stress on external evaluation
5. Predominance of criticism
6. Adult/teacher control
7. Unrewarding curriculum

Olszawski, P. et al. (1987). *The Influence of the Family Environment on the Development of Talent: A Literature Review.*

The study reviews the literature on the families of gifted and talented children to determine the importance of structural and demographic characteristics of the family, family climate and environment, and values espoused or enacted by parents. Family climate variables distinguished between individuals who evidenced creative achievement and those who evidenced academic achievement. Creatively gifted children had family environments that shared independence, were less child centered and had tense family relationship and more negative effect, resulting in motivation to attain power. Scholastic Achievers come from cohesive, child centered families with strong parent child identification.

Green, K. et al (1988). *Family Characteristics and Underachieving Gifted Adolescent Males.*

The family system of 45 underachieving and 45 achieving gifted male adolescents were compared on the variables of family functionality, family satisfaction, family environment (conflict, achievement orientation, independence, and expressiveness), and achievement satisfaction. Families with achieving and underachieving gifted students did not differ on the measures of family functionality. Achievement satisfaction and family satisfaction differentiated families on the basis of the status of their gifted children. Students' achievement satisfaction differed from functional to dysfunctional families. Families with achieving gifted students expressed higher achievement satisfaction than families with underachieving gifted students, and dysfunctional families with underachieving adolescent were less satisfied with their child's environment than were functional families with an underachieving student.

Rimm, S. & Lowe, B. (1988). *Family Environments of underachieving gifted students.*

A comparison of the family environments of a sample of twenty two underachieving gifted students to those described in studies of eminent and gifted Achievers was done and the results indicate that the family climate of Underachievers was very different from the biographical information on eminence. Although early child centeredness and liberal parenting encouraged independence and often too much power, latter parenting become inconsistent. One parent become the `mean' parent while other took the role of 'protector'.

Husband/wife relations relative to parenting were strained. Parent/child relations with at least one parent, and sometimes both parents become oppositional.

Sibling rivalry for almost half the children appeared more extreme than usual, and general relationships in the home were much more negative than those described in the biographies of Achievers. In some cases, one sibling allied himself or herself with the mother while other sibling formed an alliance with the father. In other cases, all the children in the family united with one parent against the other. In an effort to be reasonable and flexible, parents were often viewed by children as inconsistent and weak.

Baum, et al. (1995). Reversing *Underachievement: Creative Productivity and a Systematic Intervention.*

Four factors contributed to the under-achievement of the High academic achievement potential (HAP) of Underachievers. The four factors are emotional issues; social and behavioural issues; lack of appropriate curriculum; learning disabilities and poor self-regulation. Emotional issues were the most frequent primary factors, curriculum issues and learning disabilities/poor self regulation tied for second and social/behavioural concerns was the least frequent factor.

Maitre (1996). *Parenting the Gifted.*

Many of the parents because of lack of proper education are not able to guide their children from the point of view of choice of schools, choice of peer group and fail to give any sort of academic help. They, themselves, even if are motivated, are not able to give proper education or to send their children to good school because of lack of money. In some cases, they themselves are misguided. In some other cases, over exert their children from academic achievement for which the children may not have any aptitude or capabilities. So, instead of helping their children understand their problems, these parents increase their children's problems, making them emotionally vulnerable. They may set a very high goal for their children which they are not able to attain. As they are unable to find out the real reasons for their academic failure, they make their children responsible. In these cases also, the children lose all interest in school studies and drop-out of the system.

IV. Gifted Achievers and Underachievers - their personality and need achievement; personality and socio-economic status; need achievement

and socio-economic status; personality, need achievement and socio-economic status.

Haggard, E. (1957). *Socialization, personality and Academic Achievement of Gifted Children.*

The study was designed to find out interrelationships among the personality (or non-intellectual) and academic achievement variables on pre-adolescents. It was further desired to examine the socialization pattern of high and low Achievers. In the grade III high general Achievers were sensitive and responsive to socialization pressures, had largely accepted adult values and were striving to live up to adult expectations. They saw their parents as being some what over-protecting, pressuring for achievement, and lacking in emotional warmth. In their behaviour with others, they were some what more tense, competitive and aggressive, had developed good work habits and were persistent in them; got along well with their parents, teachers and peers; and showed a high level of overall adjustment than did the low academic Achievers. By grade VII, various changes had taken place in the children who remained high academic Achievers. Although they continued to respond to the socialization pressures of adults and to strive towards adult standards of behaviour, they had developed strong antagonistic attitudes towards adults and often pictured adults as being inadequate and ineffective. Such attitudes were not expressed by the low Achievers. High Achievers become more aggressive, persistent, hard-driving and competitive, and they showed signs of willingness to be aggressive and destructive in order to win over and defeat other persons. High Achievers began to emerge as the social leaders of their peers; they served at the important class committees and held important class offices and so on. Actually they were respected more than liked by their peers. The findings indicate that the groups of children who are similar in the level or pattern of academic achievement are, in many respects, also similar in a variety of personality and other non-intellectual characteristics. Children with the same intelligence quotients showed widely different pattern of academic achievement. Of the children who were exposed to roughly equivalent pressures to achieve, only a small number did so with relative ease and dispatch. Other children become tense, anxious, guilty or rebellious and performed less well than they might have under more relaxed conditions. Latter some children seemed to be on the way to becoming academic casualties of their parents' excessive ambitions for them.

Pierce, J.V. (1962). *The Bright Achiever and underachiever: A comparison.*

It was hypothesized that variability in achievement among equally able students could be accounted for in terms of differing degrees of adjustment and in differing degree of ability and willingness to adjust to the demands of the school situation. It was also pointed out that an intelligence type test required much less of a bright student than did a good in the school setting.

Two hundred and twenty two bright high school students (approximately the top 1/3 in ability) were divided into high and low achieving groups by sex and grade level. High and low achieving groups were then compared on adjustment as measured by self report instrument California Psychological Inventory (CPI); a peer rating instrument, who are they (WAT); and by a teacher rating instrument, Behaviour Description Chart (BDC).

The results were:

i. The high achieving students described themselves as being better adjusted socially; and

ii. Their peers and teachers described them as being less aggressive, maladjusted and as possessing more leadership ability. With respect to students' goals, attitudes towards school, reading habits and identifications with educationally oriented adults, the high achieving group scored higher than their comparable low achieving peer groups in all instances. High achieving boys scored somewhat higher on achievement motivation than their low achieving peers, but achievement motivation failed to differentiate for girls. Mothers of high achieving boys were found to be less authoritarian and controlling than mothers of low achieving boys. Low status, low achieving boys had mothers who were the most authoritarian and controlling of any group. While authoritarian and controlling attitudes on the part of mothers appeared to hinder their sons achievement, this did not appear to hold true for girls. Finally, mothers of high achieving boys and girls reported their children to be more responsible with respect to doing what was expected of them than did the mothers of low achieving boys and girls.

Havighurst, R. J. (1976). *Conditions Productive of Superior Children.*

Havighurst has summarized eleven characteristics of able Underachievers: (i) see themselves as inadequate persons; (ii) have lower aspirations than Achievers; (iii) do not like school as Achievers do; (iv) do not enjoy learning from books; (v) have lower popularity and leadership status in the eyes of their age mates; (vi) tend to come from homes that are broken or emotionally inadequate in other ways; (vii) come from homes of lower socioeconomic status; (viii) vocational goals are not as clearly defined as those of Achievers; (ix) have poor study habits than Achievers; (x) have narrow interests than those of Achievers; (xi) have poor adjustment than that of Achievers.

Whitemore, J. R. (1980). *Giftedness Conflict and Underachievement.*

Whitemore has summarized some of the characteristics of Underachievers as vast gap between quality level of oral and written work, consistently incomplete school work, poor execution of work, aggressive behaviour, lack of concentration, tendencies to continually set goals and standards too high, very low self-esteem and unhealthy self concept producing, difficulties in coping emotionality, lack of self-confidence, inferiority feeling, inability to function constructively in a group of any size, tendency to attribute success and failure to external control, believing he/she had no personal ability to achieve success in the classroom setting, lack of academic initiative, school phobia or complete disinterest in attendance, participation and withdrawn behaviour, no significant communication with peers or teachers.

Hussain, M.G. (1987). *Giftedness and Motivation - A study of a disadvantaged minorities.*

100 boys and girls from advantaged and disadvantaged area of Delhi, within an age range of 13-19 years studying in IX and X classes, were the sample for the study. Ravans' advanced progressive Matrices for the measurement of intelligence, Wallach and Kogan's battery of verbal creativity instruments adopted in English by Parmesh, (1972) and Hindi (Hussain, 1975) for the measurement of creativity, Rao's Achievement Motivation scale served as tools to collect the data.

The results indicate that two types of environment, i.e., advantaged and disadvantaged did not show any significant impact on the achievement motivation of the subjects. The high and low economic conditions however showed significant differences in their scores, as also did their interaction. Achievement motivation scores of the disadvantaged (economically high) was the highest followed by its advantaged counterparts. However, the two gifted groups did not show differences of any significance. The disadvantaged subjects' scores on all the three factors (intelligence, creativity and achievement motivation), showed interrelationship except creativity and intelligence. Whereas all the scores of the disadvantaged groups are found significantly correlated.

Chhaya, M.P. (1988) *Finding Gifted Children.*

Chhaya has pointed out that following are the factors related to underachievement of gifted children: (i) lack of clarity and definiteness of academic and occupational choice; (ii) weak ego control; (iii) withdrawal and self sufficiency; (iv) poor use of time and money; (v) neurotic tendencies; (vi) authoritarianism in the parental home or the individual himself; (vii) dominant and autocratic parents; (viii) impossible demands by parents; (ix) irresponsibility and lack of maturity; (x) disinterest in other people; (xi) lack of dominance and self-confidence; (xii) lack of persuasiveness; (xiii) tendency to withdraw from life.

Lidhoo M. L. and Khan, M. A. (1990). *Bright Underachievers among Socially Backward Counselling and Remedial measures.*

The study was conducted on a sample of bright Achievers and Underachievers in order to examine whether individual counselling helps to elevate the academic performance of gifted Underachievers and to study the factors which were responsible for the underachievement of bright subjects. After evaluating the results of individual counselling on the basis of pre and post test counselling data, and data got by administering the questionnaire on home background, study habits and need achievement, substantiated further by counselling sessions, it was found that bright Underachievers have poor home background, weak study habits and low need achievement. Secondly, individual counselling helped bright Underachievers to improve their scholastic achievement. The pre and past test results were statistically significant ($P < 0.05$).

McCall, et al. (1992). *High School Underachievers: What do They Achieve as Adults.*

Underachievers who were less likely to catch up to what their abilities predict had lower educational and occupational aspirations and expectations, poor self-esteem, less well-educated parents, and a stronger perception that external, rather than personal, factors controlled their lives than youths with the same grades

Collectively, these characteristics suggest that Underachievers have lower perceived competence relative to their grades, and perhaps as a consequence, they lack the disposition to persist at educational, occupational, and personal tasks in the face of challenge.

McCough, D.B. and Siegle Del (2003). *Factors that Differentiate Underachieving Gifted Students from High-Achieving Gifted Students.*

The purpose of this study was to examine whether gifted Achievers and gifted Underachievers differ in their general academic self-perceptions, attitudes toward school, attitudes toward teachers, motivation and self-regulation, and goal valuation. The sample consisted of 56 gifted Underachievers and 122 gifted Achievers from 28 high schools nation-wide. Gifted Achievers and gifted Underachievers differed in their attitudes toward school, attitude toward teachers, motivation/self-regulation and goal valuation, but not their academic self-perceptions. In addition, the logistic regression analysis correctly classified over 81 % of the sample as either gifted Achievers or gifted Underachievers using their motivation/self regulation and goal valuation self-ratings. This study represents an important step toward quantifying factors related to the underachievement of gifted adolescents.

General Conclusion

I. So far as the studies conducted in India are concerned, except a few well-known foreign tools like Wechsler's Intelligence Scale, Ravens Advanced progressive Matrices, Cattell's personality Questionnaires and Thematic Apperception Test, etc, continue to be used. It is generally encouraging that researchers have increasingly started employing the tools developed by either themselves or Indian psychologists and educators.

II. A trend that emerges out of the related literature is that maximum researches carried out are descriptive in nature. The researchers have selected some variables to study their relations with achievement. Mostly correlational techniques and `t' test have been used or at the best analysis of variance. The sophisticated techniques of factor analysis or co-variance have been rarely used.

III. The review of literature specifies that the criteria for academic achievement has been considered to be the scores (marks) gained by sample subjects in the previous examination. It is noteworthy that at the time of examination various extraneous variables would operate and influence the academic achievement.

IV. All the factors of Personality and Need Achievement have not been dealt by the researchers in general. And there is not a complete agreement among the researchers on the high/low socio-economic status of gifted Achievers and under-Achievers.

V. Among the studies reviewed, no study has investigated the effect of all variables, namely, Personality Factors, Need Achievement and Socio-economic Status on Academic Achievement of the gifted Achievers and Underachievers. Moreover, it is believed that once some of the important factors are given a chance to interplay and interact, new situations are likely to emerge (Allport 1973). This is exactly what is in the mind of the author and the study has proceeded on these lines.

Methodology and Procedure

A man who does not think and plan long ahead will find trouble right at his door.

Confucius

Van Dalen (1973) has aptly remarked that research is not to be divided into water tight compartments. He states, "Research is often a confused, floundering process rather than a logical, orderly one. An investigator does not tackle one step at a time, complete that process, and then move on the next step. He may tackle the steps out of order, shuffle back and forth between steps, or work on two steps more or less simultaneously..., when the investigator reports his findings to the scientific community, however, he structures his presentation in a precise and logically arranged form which closely paralles the steps of the scientific method" (P-14). Thoughtlessness in designing any research proposal leads to blind alleys and renders the research effort futile. Kothari (1990) observes that the research design must make enough provisions for protection against bias and must minimize reliability, with due concern to the economical completion of the study. Kerlinger (1986) holds that research designs are invented to enable researchers to answer research questions as validly, objectively, accurately and economically as possible. Research plans are deliberately and specifically conceived and executed to bring empirical evidence to the problem in question. The ideas of different authors make it obvious that it is only the appropriate design which sifts the facts in the light of objectives and enables the researcher to achieve results.

In the light of above description and keeping in view the various research designs discussed by Hopkins (1976), Goldman (1978), Travers (1978), Tuckman (1978), Best (1983), suitable for different problems, the present investigator followed the following steps in the preparation of the research design, which is descriptive and diagnostic in nature, in order to achieve logical conclusions.

I. Formation of objectives:

The objectives for the present study have been framed and given in chapter - I

II. The sample:

In District Anantnag there are five Tehsils. Out of five Tehsils, one Tehsil (Anantnag) was dropped because of its semi-urban bias. Secondly, out of remaining four Tehsils, two Tehsils (Kulgam and Duroo) were (randomly) dropped in order to make the study manageable within the stipulated time.

All the male subjects studying in class 9th and 10th within an age range of 14 to 16 were contacted from the Govt. High and Higher Secondary Schools of two Tehsils (Pahalgam and Bijbehara) of District Anantnag. Govt. Higher Secondary School Bijbehara was dropped from being a sample unit because of its semi-urban bias. Private schools were not considered as sample units because

i) They do not follow the same curriculum;

ii) Teacher recruitment is guided by their own recruitment policy;

iii) The conducting of examination is governed by their own rules and regulations;

iv) The students reading in these schools decidedly possess a high socio-economic status.

It would have certainly affected the criterion variable (academic achievement). The Govt. Schools more or less possess a uniformity, therefore, objective results are expected. Sex was also controlled to avoid gender differences in results. The choice of the 9th and 10th class subjects was based on the rationale that the students of this age group are superior to the students of lower classes (8th...Ist) in maturity and judgement.

a) Initial sample:

Following is the institution wise distribution of initial sample:

Name of the Institution	Class wise No. of subjects		Total No. of subjects	Students Dropped	Net sample
	9th	10th			
H. S. Sallar	58	60	118	-	118
H. S. Kathsoo	23	26	49	-	49
H.S.S. Sriguphwara	65	61	126	-	126
H. S. Khrim	52	47	99	-	99
H.S. Mahind	94	46	140	01	139
H. S. Nainal	50	79	129	01	128
H.S. Marhama	32	34	66	-	66
H. S. Pahalgam	21	16	37	-	37
H.S. Batkote	11	12	23	-	33
H.S. Aishmukam	71	39	110	-	110
H.S. Selia	42	54	96	-	96
H.S. S. Mattan	117	95	212	03	209
Total	**636**	**569**	**1205**	**05**	**1200**

Thus the initial sample comprised of 1200 subjects.

b) Final sample

A non-verbal mental measurement test-Ravens Advanced progressive Matrics (1962) was administered to all the 1200 sample subjects in different sittings, after building a rapport with the subjects and the concerned principals and teachers of respective schools. The subjects scoring above 80th percentile (14.95=15) on the I.Q. test were termed as gifted (N=267). The institution wise distribution of final sample is cited as follows:

Name of the Institution	Total No. of subjects	No. of subjects whose achievement was not available	Class wise No. of subjects		Students Dropped	Net sample
			9th	10th		
H. S. Sallar	38	01	14	23	-	37
H. S. Kathsoo	08	-	04	04	-	08
H.S.S. Sriguphwara	05	-	03	02	-	05
H. S. Khrim	11	-	02	09	-	11
H.S. Mahind	12	-	06	06	-	11
H. S. Nanil	23	-	06	17	01	22
H.S.Marhama	15	01	03	11	05	09
H. S. Pahalgam	06	-	04	02	-	06
H.S. Batkote	09	-	3	6	2	07
H.S. Aishmukam	34	-	14	20	01	33
H.S. Selia	31	01	08	22	12	18
H.S.S. Mattan	75	04	22	49	11	60

Out of 267 subjects 07 subjects were screened out because their academic achievement was not available in their respective schools, where they had read previously as the schools were burnt due to the disturbed conditions in the valley. Another 32 subjects were also dropped from the remaining 260 subjects, as some subjects had dropped out of the school and others had given fictitious or incomplete responses to the tests administered to them. Therefore, in the final analysis the investigator was left with 228 subjects which served as the sample for the study. The mean of the previous two annual examination results (7th and 8th for 9th class students and 8th and 9th for 10th class students) was considered as a criterion for academic achievement. Subjects whose achievement scores were 10 percentile and above of their intelligence percentile scores were considered as gifted Achievers and the subjects whose achievement scores were 10 percentile or more below their intelligence percentile scores were considered as gifted under-Achievers. The criterion model is in line with Gowan (1960) which has successfully been used by Mohan and Nehru (1972). Mohan and Khera (1978). The intelligence and Achievement percentile scores of sample subjects are given as follows:-

Respective percentile of scores on intelligence (I.Q. Test and Academic Achievement.

Percentiles pp	**I.Q. Scores**	**Academic achievement score**
	Lowest score = 15	Lowest score = 19
P10	15.15 = 15	24.44 = 24
P20	15.9 = 16	28.5 = 29
P30	16.84 = 17	31.83 = 32
P40	17.81 = 18	35.01 = 35
P50	18.58 = 19	38.03 = 38
P60	19.60 = 20	41.25 = 41
P70	20.53 = 21	44.88 =45
P80	21.54 = 22	48.75 = 49
P90	22.9 = 23	57.15 = 57
	Highest score = 26	Highest score = 73

Following the criterion model 128 subjects out of 228 were termed as gifted Achievers and the remaining (100) were termed as gifted Underachievers.

In order to make it sure that two gifted groups – gifted Achievers and gifted Underachievers differ significantly so far as their achievement is concerned, 't' test was employed and the table for the same is given below:

Table 01: Significance of Mean difference between gifted Achievers (N=128) and Underachievers (N=100) so far as their achievement is concerned.

	$\bar{X}$	σ	SED	't' value
Gifted Achievers	46.91	7.55	1.00	15.46**
Gifted under-Achievers	31.45	7.45		

The perusal of the above table makes it clear that gifted Achievers and Underachievers differ significantly so far as their achievement is concerned. Thus the two gifted groups are decidedly poles apart so far as their achievement is concerned. Therefore, it is further substantiated that the use of criterion model for identification of gifted achieves and Underachievers is an objective one.

III. Collecting the Data with appropriate tools:

Selection of tools imposes a high premium on the outcome of knowledge. If the tools are devoid of any precision, accuracy and relevance, the researcher is bound to land into blind alleys and come out with faulty inference. It is not possible that one single tool or device can work as panacca and help in achieving all the objectives under investigation. Keeping such limitations in view, the present investigator made a comprehensive study of various tools as mentioned in the sixth Mental Measurement Yearbook of Buro's (1965) and the First Mental Measurement Yearbook by Long and Mehta (1966). Besides the review of related literature developed an insight in the mind of the investigator to select the relevant tools for the collection of required data. Below are mentioned the tools which were adopted for the collection of data.

01. Ravens Advanced Progressive Matrices (1962)

Most of the tests of Mental Measurement in the world are standardized on English speaking/knowing population and in India, either on English or Hindi knowing population. Therefore, it was not desirable to select any verbal test as the sample because the subjects were not conversant with these languages. To overcome this difficulty a non-verbal test of mental measurement, Ravens Advanced Progressive Materices (1962), was considered an adequate tool to get an Index of the I.Q. of the sample subjects.

Description of the test:

The objectives for the construction of the advanced progressive Matrices (APM) was to build a non-verbal test for the establishment of intellectual differences among the intellectually dull, average and bright.

It comprises two sets of problems: Set I and Sec II. In Set I there are 12 pictorial problems designed to introduce a person to the method of working and covers all the intellectual processes needed for success. The first problem is as nearly as possible self-evident. The problems become difficult progressively. In Set II there are 36 pictorial problems in presentation and argument. These problems are identical with those in Set I. They only increase in difficulty more steadily and become considerably more complex. To avoid fatigue and boredom, the figures are drawn boldly and accurately and these are pleasing for assessing a person's maximum capacity to form comparisons and reason analogy, without being unduly exhausted. The scale is self-administered or can be administered to an individual or a group at a time. A person's total score in Set II provides an index of one's intellectual capacity. The test is being used throughout the world.

Administration and scoring:

The test was administered in different sittings to the sample subjects so as to increase objectivity and keep a firm vigil on them. The sample subjects were seated comfortably, mostly in the school ground, sufficiently apart, facing the investigator in order to avoid copying. After distributing the answer sheets, they were asked to fill up the particulars themselves in the answer sheet and were instructed not to open the booklet (Set I) until every one was ready. The investigator explained the problems of set I and the ways of answering them correctly. After sound instructions set I was administered and after a break of five minutes set II in order to avoid monotony. The scoring of the answer sheets was done strictly in accordance with the scoring key of the manual (APM. 1962).

02. Urdu Adaptation of Jr. Sr. High School personality Questionnaire

Though there is no paucity of tests in personality, developed in India and abroad, yet no other test covers all the major dimensions of personality to describe individual differences comprehensively. It deals with psychologically meaningful and productively important traits that have demonstrable functional unity, and are central to any discussion in general psychological theory. Cattell (1976, p. 05) observes that it is the characteristic feature of H.S.P.Q. that by adding measures on this comprehensive series of personality measurement, the psychologist is able to increase in fact (just about the double) the accuracy of predictions of school achievement obtained from the intelligence scores. It is the test which gives the teacher an insightful understanding and qualitative evaluation of those aspects of a particular pupil's personality, contributing to, or distracting from, his performance in school and his social adjustment inside and outside the classroom. The complete profile of fourteen personality factors are equally relevant to child guidance, counselling and classroom purposes.

Keeping the above given facts in view Jr. Sr. HSPQ was considered an appropriate tool for the measurement of personality dimensions. As the test is devised in English, it was not possible for the present investigator to use the test in the same language. The sample subjects were Kashmiri speaking and had command on Urdu language only. Therefore, the test was translated into Urdu language in order to achieve logical and objective conclusions. The scheme of translating the test is mentioned as follows:-

I. Firstly, the test was translated from English to Urdu by the present investigator;

II. Secondly, for further improvement in the draft, an expert consultancy was sought from the Department of Urdu, Kashmir University;

III. Thirdly, a panel of 10 judges was selected by the present investigator, in consultation with the Supervisor and the Head of the Department, to make it sure that each item of the translated version conveys the same meaning as the items in the original scale. The judges were requested to rate their opinion either Perfectly Agree (PA) or Perfectly Disagreed (PD) or Not Agree (NA). In case a judge did not agree with the feasibility of any translated item, he was requested to suggest the change. A jury of ten experts, conversant with both English and Urdu languages, were selected on the pretax:

a) Dr. Madhosh, Dr. Tantray, Dr. Zargar and Dr. Malik from the field of Education and Psychology;

b) Dr. Maliki; Dr. Andrabi and Dr. Muzamir from the field of Urdu language;

c) Dr. Maliki, Dr. Tak and Dr. Hamida from the field of English language.

IV. Fourthly, the items, on which there was the consensus of 08 judges and above, were retained as such and no change was inserted. The items, on which there was a consensus of seven or less No. of judges, were changed in accordance with the suggested change of the judges. Thus the translated test has 0.8 as the validity co-efficient. And it can be said with firmness that the items on translated version convey the same meaning as on original English one.

V. In order to establish further that the Urdu translated version represents the original English one, the Urdu version was administered to a sample of 30 subjects who were conversant with both the languages. It needs mention, that the sample subjects belonged to a private school situated in Srinagar, namely, CASET School, Karanagar, and were within the age range of 15-16. After a lapse of two months the English version was administered to the same subjects. Finally the correlation by product moment was computed between first and second test results. The factor wise co-efficient of correlation is presented in the table 02 as follows:

Table 02

A	B	C	D	E	F	G	H	I	J	O	Q_2	Q_3	Q_4
.84	.83	.86	.83	.71	.78	.70	.81	.79	.89	.78	.67	.75	.72

All the correlation coefficients are significant beyond 0.01 levels. Therefore, it substantiates that there is no need of changing the norms of the test.

Reliability

The test-retest reliability index of the scale (Urdu version) computed on 400 high school students of Kashmir after an interval of two months, is as under:-

Factors	Pearson's 'r'	Factors	Pearson's 'r'
A	0.81	H	0.84
B	0.91	I	0.83
C	0.72	J	0.79
D	0.79	O	0.82
E	0.88	Q2	0.75
F	0.73	Q3	0.88
G	0.79	Q4	0.76

Description of the test:

It is desirable in schools to screen out for individual attention and guidance those individuals who need help with emotional conflicts and behaviour disorders; or to locate individuals with unusual temperamental sensitivity, needing careful handling. By this early recognition, many behaviour difficulties can be avoided or handled before they harden into defensive habits and complications resistive to treatment. Psychologists like Catell et al., (1961) and Wright (1955) have observed that school achievement can be more exactly predicted and understood when appropriately weighted personality measures like HSPQ are used in addition to the usual ability measures. It is an instrument that gives an objective analysis of the individual personality to supplement, the teacher's personal evaluation. The test is primarily intended for an age range of 12 through 18.

It is a trichotomised "yes" "uncertain" "No" response pattern measuring fourteen factors – ten items per factor plus two buffer items. Each of the fourteen personality dimensions measured by HSPQ has a professional, popular and alphabetic designation, besides universal index number. The HSPQ enjoys a high degree of reliability and validity fully described in the manual and Handbook of the HSPQ. Table 03 presents a full factor by factor listing and description of the fourteen dimensions as measured by HSPQ. Each factor is presented as a bipolar continuum with bipolar titles.

Table 03: Titles and symbols for designating the fourteen dimensions.

		Low Sten Score Description (1-3)	*	High Sten Score Description (8-10)	
Professional Term Popular Terms	(A-)	Sizothymia Reserved, detached, critical, aloof, stiff	A	Affectoth-ymia Warm-hearted, outgoing, easy going, participating	(A+)
Professional Popular	(B-)	Low intelligence (Crystallized Power measure) Dull	B	High intelligence (Crystallized, power measure) Bright	(B+)
Professional Popular	(C-)	Lower ego strength affected by feeling emotionally less stable, easily upset changeable	C	High ego-strength, Emotionally stable mature, faces, reality, calm	(A+)

*Alphabetic designation of Factor

Professional Popular	(D-)	Phlegmatic temperament undemonstrative deliberate, inactive, stodgy	D	Excitability Excitable, Impatient, demanding overactive, unrestrained	(D+)
Professional Popular	(E-)	Submissiveness Obedient, mild, Easily led, docile accommodating	E	Dominance Assertive, Aggressive, Competitive stubborn	(E+)
Professional Popular	(F-)	Desurgency Sober, taciturn, Serious	F	Surgency Enthusiastic, heedless, happy-go-lucky	(F+)
Professional Popular	(G-)	Weaker super ego Strength Disregards rules, expedient	G	Sronger super-ego strength conscientious, persistent, moralistic, staid	(G+)
Profesional Popular	(H-)	Threctia Shy, timid threat – sensitive	H	Parmia Adventurous, thick-skinned, socially bold	(H+)
Professional Popular	(I-)	Harria Tough-minded, rejects illusions	I	Premsia Tender-minded, sensitive, dependent, over protected	(I+)
Professional Popular	(J-)	Zeppia Zestful, liking group action	J	Coasthenia Circumspect individualis, reflective, internally restrained	(J+)

Professional Popular	(O-)	Untroubled adequacy self-assured, placid, secure, complacent, serene	O	Guilt proneness Apprehensive, self reproching, insecure, worrying, troubled	(O+)
Professional Popular	(Q2-)	Group dependency Sociable group dependent, a 'joiner' and sound follower	Q2	Self-sufficiency Self-sufficient resourceful, prefers own decisions	(Q2+)
Professional Popular	(Q3-)	Low self sentiment integration, uncontrolled, lax, follows own urges, careless and social rules	Q3	High strength of self-sentiment Controlled, exacting will power, socially precise, compulsive, following self image	(Q3+)
Professional Popular	(Q4-)	Low generic tension relaxed, tranquil, torpid, unfrustrated, composed	Q4	High energic tension, Tense driven, over-wrought, fretful	(Q4+)

Administration and Scoring:

Jr. Sr. HSPQ is planning for administration in groups as well as individually. The test is administered without a time limit and can be completed by all but the slowest readers in about 40-50 minutes per form. In the present study the HSPQ was administered in small groups, mostly in the school ground, with reasonable distance from one sample subject to the other, so as to avoid copying. The sample subjects were comfortably seated and after a proper rapport building in a friendly manner the test was administered.

The sample subjects were provided with a booklet HSPQ form A (Urdu Adaptation) and an answer sheet. The instructions were read aloud by the present investigator, pausing to remind the examiners to answer the examples. It was made sure that each subject had understood the way of responding to the test, which was substantiated by examining individually whether they had responded correctly to the two examples cited on the cover page. When the present investigator was sure that they had filled in the required information on the top of the answer sheet and had understood the way of responding, the sample subjects were instructed to start with the first question. During the test the meaning of words was explained to an examinee upon request, except for the intelligence scale items (23, 24, 43, 44, 63, 64, 83, 84 , 104 and 124). The test was completed by the sample subjects within fifty minutes except in certain exceptional cases whom it took 60 minutes to complete the questionnaire.

The answer sheet is scored either by (a) hand stencil key or (b) a machine. For the machine scoring, special answer sheets must be used. IN the present study, hand stencil key was used to score the answer sheets. Before scoring it was checked that each question had been given one and only one answer. Those answer sheets were screened out which were marked mechanically by the sample subjects either all right hand or left hand responses, besides all positions. Two scoring keys were used: one covers factors – A, C, E, G, I, O, Q3 and the other covers B, D, F, H, J, Qe and Q4 factors. Each answer scores 'O', 01 and '02' points except factor 'B which scores 'O' (correct) and '01' (incorrect). The 'O' is rendered invisible by the key and the visible 'O' or '2' positions are marked and weighted on the holed stencil cardboard key itself. While administering the questionnaire or scoring the answer sheets, instructions were given in the Handbook of HSPQ were strictly followed.

03. Urdu Adaptation of incomplete sentences blank (ISB) for the measurement of need achievement (N-Ach).

The concept of primary biological drive (thirst, hunger, procreation) is used to explain most of the behaviour in animal world. Human beings, on the other hand, are motivated by the needs which are not necessarily biological in nature. The concept of secondary drive is used by psychologists to explain man's different aspects of behaviour. One such drive, the motive to achieve or N.Ach is the most important of them.

To measure this secondary drive (N-Ach) among the sample subjects, so as to get an awareness about the causes of underachievement, ISB Urdu Adaptation by the present investigator was selected with the rationale:

I. That other projective tests of N-Ach like TAT comprise different pictures on cards and the respondent has to build a story on each card, which is a time consuming process. It was not possible for the present investigator to meet each student individually and administer the test because of the restriction of time.

II. Secondly, the sample subjects were from rural Kashmir. Though the test can be administered in small groups by making use of a projector, yet it was not possible to make use of such a device in remote villages in the absence of electric supply. It would have otherwise affected the test results in the form of measurement of time spent by each sample subject in the completion of each story.

III. Thirdly, the concurrent validity of ISB, used in the collection of data for the N-Ach in the present study, with TAT is 0.91 (Shah, 1977) which is beyond the significance level.

IV. Fourthly, the scoring method employed in ISB is simple, objective and does not demand for much training and sophistication, as is necessary for TAT protocols for N.Ach.

The ISB is devised in English language, it was not justified for the present investigator to administer the test as such. Further, the sample subjects were not conversant with English language as well as Kashmiri. As a matter of fact, the test was translated into Urdu language and the scheme of translation has been followed in the same manner as in Jr. Sr. HSPQ. In order to rate each item for the feasibility of each translated item from English to Urdu.

In order to validate it further, the Urdu translated version represents the original English one. The urdu translated version was administered to a sample of 30 subjects and after a lapse of two months, the English version was administered to the same sample (as was done in the case of Jr. Sr. JSPQ). Finally after the administration of both, the translated and original one, the correlation by product moment was computed between first and second test scores. The factor wise and total composite score co-efficient of correlation is presented in the table 04, as follows:

Table 4: Co-efficient of correlation factor-wise and on total composite score between English and Urdu version (N=30) after an expiry of two months.

Factor	A	B	C	D	E	G	Total composite score
'r' value	.83	.90	.85	.76	.81	.92	.91

All the correlation coefficients are significant beyond 0.01 level. Therefore, it substantiates that there is no need of changing the norms of the test.

Reliability

The test-retest reliability index of the scale (Urdu version) computed on 400 high school student's of Kashmir after an interval of two months, is as under:-

Factors	Pearson's 'r'
A	0.82
B	0.89
C	0.84
D	0.77
E	0.80
G	0.91
Total composite score	0.90

Description of the Tool:

Incomplete sentence blank (ISB) is a kind of projective test in which the respondent is required to complete a No. of sentences. A word of a part of the sentence constitutes the test item and the testee is required to write whatever comes to his mind after reading the given part of a sentence so as to complete the sentence meaningfully. The underlying assumption is that the subjects ideas and the needs are revealed by the type of responses he makes in completing the incomplete sentences. Mukherjee's ISB purports to measure only one specific area of motivation – need for achievement. The need for achievement is defined operationally as behaviour which shows efforts to do ones best or to excel others. The ISB developed by Mukherjee has been specifically constructed to assess that aspect of personality which an individual manifests in connection with his striving in the upward fashion to achieve something very significant, unique and important.

ISB consists of 71 items out of which 11 serve as filler items. Items numbering 9, 16, 28, 36, 37, 44, 52, 55, 57, 59 and 71 are the filler items. Some items of ISB incorporate stem in the first person and few items stem in the third person.

The item stems of ISB are neither too long nor too short. Each incomplete blank is of such an optimal length that a person with high need achievement (N-Ach) will tend to complete it in the keyed direction. The stems neither put excessive restrictions on the part of the testee to respond in a specific way nor evoke unlimited number of possible answers. The use of filler items and stems in third person makes the test far less transparent than many standard personality inventories. The ISB can be administered 8n groups for measuring those bipolar dimensions of personality which together constitute N-Ach, hope of success vs fear of failures; interval vs external control of fate; realistic vs unrealistic attitude high vs low ego ideal; etc. ISB-a multidimensional measure of N-Ach. measures following dimensions of N-Ach:-

A) Hope of success, with sub areas: (i) optimism; (ii) Identification with a successful authority; (iii) preference for intrinsic reward when successful.

B) High ego ideal, with sub – areas: (i) High level of aspiration; (ii) High self confidence (iii) A sense of striving to achieve a high position, status etc; (iv) competitiveness; (v) Maintenance of self-respect.

C) Perseverance, with sub-areas: (i) Persistence, Diligence etc. (ii) Preference for difficult and challenging tasks; (iii) Sense of devotion to work; (iv) Satisfaction in completing an assigned task; (v) Long term involvement with a future career; (vi) Dislike for idealness.

D) Realistic attitude, with sub-areas: (i) Intermediate risks (04 to 08 feet for item 42); (ii) Realistic aspiration; (iii) Advance planning.

E) Internal Control of Fate, with sub-areas: (i) Reliance on self-effort; (ii) Denying the role of some superior unknown force in shaping one's destiny; (iii) Strong determination.

F) Evasiveness – No. of items not responded (including filler items).

G) Incomplete – No. of items not completed meaningfully (including filler items).

Administration and Scoring:

The sample subjects were seated comfortably in the school ground apart from each other so as to avoid copying. The ISB (Urdu adaptation) was administered in different sittings. It was explained to the subjects that the ISB is not a vocabulary test but a simple tool for measuring how rapidly and frankly you complete the blanks. The instructions were read aloud by the present investigator on the face sheet of ISB carefully, in order to acquaint the subjects with the pattern of completing the stems. The subjects were instructed that there is no time limit for the test, however, each of the blank should be filled in as quickly as possible. It was made sure to the subjects that their responses will remain strictly confidential and were instructed to feel at ease and be honest.

The ISB protocols are presently being scored on the basis of the presence or absence of certain aspects of achievement motivation. Each response is scored either +1 or –1 depending upon what manifest or latent need the complete sentence reflected. Each complete sentence is scored as +1 provided it indicates any of the above given aspect of N-Ach, If the responses reflect the opposite of the areas of N-Ach, it is scored as –1, e.g., sentences reflecting fear of failure in place of hope of success and the like. Scoring of 11 items (09, 16, 28, 36, 37, 44, 52, 55, 57, 59, and 71) is not done, for these items are regarded as filler items. Responses indicating other areas of manifest needs such as affiliation, nurturance, exhibitionism, sex etc. are scored as zero. The total score is the algebraic sum of all the positive and negative scores received in the total test comprising of 60 items. For the items which have not been completed fully or not attempted at all, the respondent receives a score of zero on each of the five dimensions. However, he is given a score of 01 for incompleteness. In extreme cases of evasiveness or incompleteness, the protocols should be, however, discarded unless it involves a psychiatric case study (Mukherjee, 1977).

Reliability:

The odd-even reliability of the ISB, excluding the 11 filler items, has been found to be 0.65 for a sample of 180 post graduate students of Nagpur University. The internal consistence reliability computed by the Kuder-Richardson formula 20 from the item analysis results based on 100 subjects turned out to be 0.61.

Validity:

The product moment correlation between ISB and a force choice scale of achievement values called the sentence completion test Mukjerjee, (1964) is .235, on a sample of 100 Nagpur University Post-graduate students. The ISB is also validate with TAT in Kashmir by Shah, (1977) and the correlation co-efficient by product moment is 0.91 which is significant beyond .01 level.

Administration and Scoring:

The Urdu Adaptation of Need Achievement was administered to sample subjects in different sittings. Scoring of the test was done strictly according to the instructions in the manual.

04. Kashmiri Adaptation of Socio-economic status scale(Rural) Pareek and Trivedi by the present investigator.

Though there are various standardized scales of socio-economic status (SES) available in India, on rural population like Lewis and Dillon (1955), Freeman (1961), yet the scale devised by Pareek and Trivedi (1964) is relatively appropriate for the measurement of SES on the rural sample. In Kashmir no such scale on SES had been constructed earlier to the present investigation on rural population. The present investigator thoroughly analysed the scale of Pareek and Trivedi and there were many limitations in it. The limitations are cited as under:-

i) the scale is very old devised in 1964 and the SES of the people has considerably risen;

ii) the most important component of SES – Income is missing in the scale;

iii) the item of vital importance now-a-days in order to determine ones SES – like education and occupation of the mother are again missing;

iv) Horticulture land which is the back-bone of Kashmiri economy and has a vital role to play so as to determine ones SES is conspicuous by its absence;

v) The people of Kashmir are also rich enough to possess many more material things that provide a distinctive status to people. It becomes more pertinent as the facilitates of life have changed from 1964 to date enormously. Therefore, restricting the Material possessing to only a few things, as are in the scale is not justified;

vi) The scale has a different cultural bias and has not been standardized in respect of Kashmir population;

vii) The sixth sub-head of the item of occupation - service, has not been categorized;

viii) As the facilities of higher education have increased and an awareness for education has achieved a momentum in the rural areas either, leaving the item of education on 9th sub-head (graduation) is not justified now-a-days.

Keeping the above limitations in view the present investigator, in consultation with the experts in the field, thought it advisable to make the Kashmiri adaptation of the scale. The item wise adaptation is cited as under:-

i) Caste: The second sub-head of the caste item represented by lower caste, is appropriate for the Hindus only. But so far as the Muslims are concerned, we cannot attribute a person to be of a caste which is lower, therefore, sub-head lower caste was rewritten as lower caste/social caste, so as to make it meaningful for the Muslims.

ii) Occupation: So far as the occupation item is concerned it is attributed to the head of the family-father, or guardian, in favour of those whose father is dead. But so far as the present scenario is concerned the occupation of the mother adds to the family income and provides a better socioeconomic status to the family. Therefore, the 'occupation of Mother' item was added. The item of occupation of Father was made more clear by categorizing the service sub-head.

iii) Education: The education of the head of the family is ascertained for the component of education, in order to represent educational status. But education of the mother is equally important in determining the status of the family. Therefore, the education of mother item was included in the adapted form. The item of education of father was changed.

iv) The item of Monthly income is added in the adopted version, that is not represented in the original scale.

v) Social Participation: The item was placed in the adapted version as such.

vi) Land: In the original scale there was not the categorization of land agriculture and Horticulture. Therefore, it was categorized so as to represent Agriculture and Horticulture land separately in two items. After the land reform act was implemented in Kashmir, the land possession has shrunk to the minimum level. Therefore, the range of land as placed in the original scale was subdivided into two halves, Agriculture and Horticulture.

vii) In rural Kashmir the Gujars live in far flung areas in hutment's commonly termed as Kothas. Therefore, the second sub item- Hut was rewritten as Hut/Kotha.

viii) Farm Power: This item was replaced by farm power and animal possession as in the rural area of Kashmir, people not only possess drought and prestige animals but also gercy cows and sheep. It certainly adds to the status of a family. Therefore, animal possession was also included in this item.

ix) Material Possession: As the people throughout India are materially more sound than in 1964, therefore, some new additions were made in this item. As in Kashmir there is not an existence of bullock cart, therefore, the sub-item was re-phased as Bullcart

cart/Horse cart. As in certain areas Horse carts are plying on the roads, the sub head of improved agriculture implements was rewritten as improved agricultural implements/ spray machine.

x) Family: The family item was placed as such no change was inserted.

Content Validity:

After the additions and alterations of the original scales was worked out, a jury of ten experts was selected to act as judges in order to validate the Kashmiri adaptation of socioeconomic status scale. The judges were provided with the original scale and the adapted one and a form to record their agreement or dis-agreement on any of the items or sub head of items changed or added. Judges were requested to examine the changed version critically and suggest changes wherever necessary. They were also requested that while evaluating the adapted scale and comparing it with the original one, the weightage assigned to each item and sub head should also be considered. They were also requested to show their disagreement, if they did not agree with the feasibility of an added item or sub head of an item in the changed version.

Wherever the judges had felt a necessity, they had recorded their disagreement and suggested the change. In the same vein wherever it was felt that weightage is given more or less, the change was suggested by the experts. Thus, as a matter of fact the additions and alterations were made in the adapted scale in the following manner:-

i) If there was the consensus of eight or nine judges, on the addition of an item or sub head of an item, the item or sub head of an item was retained.

ii) If there was the agreement of eight or more judges on the change of the item or sub head of an item, the change in the changed version was retained.

iii) If there was the consensus of seven or less No. of judges on the addition of an item or sub head of an item, the idea of addition was dropped.

iv) If there was only agreement of seven or less No. of judges on the change of an item or sub head of an item, the idea of changing the item or sub head of an item (in the original scale) was dropped.

v) The weightage of an item or sub head of an item was retained as such when eight or more No. of judges expressed their agreement. The weightage was changed when there was the agreement of only 07 or les No. of judges.

The perusal of the above description makes it clear that the adapted version has a co-efficient of 0.08 as its content validity.

Item Analysis:

The changed version of SES scale was administered to 120 subjects, randomly selected from the Tehsils Pahalgam and Bijbehara. The scripts were scored and arranged in ascending order based on the total score obtained by the sample subjects. Thirty scripts getting the highest score (top 25%) and 30 scripts getting the lowest score (lowest 25%) were taken to form the upper and lower groups. For the purpose of item, analysis these two groups served as criterion groups. The criterion model is in line with Madhosh and Rafiqui (1990). The discriminatory power of each item was detected by the score obtained for each item by these two groups. x and S.D. was computed for each item in both the groups (high and low). Finally 't' test was used to select the item for the final draft of this scale. The item analysis was done only for the items which were included afresh – Mother's education, Mothers occupation, Income, land Horticulture, and the items where there was a marked change-land agriculture, occupation Father, education Father, Farm power and animal possession, Material possession. After computing item analyses of these items all were retained as the 't' value was significant beyond 0.05 level, on each of the item as shown in table 05.

Table 5: Item analysis of the composite score of SES, the items added afresh and the items changed (High and low group N=30 each).

Variables	Groups	$\bar{x}$	S.D.	't' value
"01"				
Composite score	High	40.17	4.71	17.19**
SES	Low	23.60	2.37	
"02"				
Occupation	High	5.67	1.69	4.09**
Father	Low	4.03	1.38	
"03"				
Occupation	High	2.20	1.22	2.41**
Mother	Low	1.60	0.61	
"04"				
Education	High	3.73	1.82	8.39**
Father	Low	0.43	1.15	
"05"				
Education	High	1.07	1.89	2.97**
Mother	Low	0.03	1.79	
"06"				
Monthly	High	4.43	0.88	6.62**
Income	Low	2.70	1.13	

"08" Land Agriculture	High	2.77	1.31	4.22**
	Low	1.53	0.92	
"09" Land Horticulture	High	1.80	1.83	3.43**
	Low	0.57	0.75	
"11" Farm Power & Animal Possession	High	3.87	1.99	3.06**
	Low	2.47	1.52	
"12" Material Possession	High	4.10	2.76	4.11**
	Low	1.87	1.12	

** Probability less than 0.01
* Probability less than 0.05.

Reliability:

The co-efficient of stability was calculated for the present scale by the test –retest method. The coefficient of correlation of the scale scores, by product moment method, taken at two different times, within a time duration of two months, on thirty persons selected randomly from different villages, indicated quite a high coefficient of stability – 0.91. The selection of the sample subjects was done randomly from 10 high and higher secondary schools reading in 9th class (three subjects from each institution).

Norms

The researchers are free to make use of raw scores for comparison purposes in groups But for more precise interpretation, comparison and for research purposes the use of norms is recommended. The norms given here were developed on the data collected from the villages of District Anantnag (N=950).

The norms can be used in comparable areas of the state. For the present scale (Kashmiri adaptation), percentile norms have been worked out. A percentile indicates an individual's relative position in the standardized sample. Percentiles serve as ranks in the group of 100 when we begin from the bottom so that the lower the percentile, the lower the individuals status. Following the principle of proportionate division, a raw score falling in between the cut off points can suitably be converted into percentile scores.

Table 6: Percentile norms of Kashmiri adaptation of socio-economic status scale (N=95).

Percentile points	Scores
	High score = 61
P90	42.32
P80	37.42
P70	35.10
P60	32.79
P50	30.91
P40	29.15
P30	27.25
P20	25.45
P10	23.42
	Lowest score = 14

The investigator has also made an arbitrary classification of the scores for identifying some explanatory categories. For this purpose three point scale has been used. The first high socio-economic group (upper class), second average socio-economic group (middle class) and the Third low socio-economic group (lower class). These groups were obtained by taking P25, P75 for upper and lower class (extreme groups, and the score rànging between P25 and P75 for middle class. The data is given in the table 7 as under:-

Table 7: Representation of scores and respective classes on socio-economic status (N=950)

Class	Score
Upper	36.18 and above
Middle	26.36+ to 36.17
Lower	26:35 and below

Administration and Scoring

The sample subjects were seated comfortably in the school ground apart from each other and the Kashmiri Adaptation of socio-economic status scale was administered in different sittings. It was explained to the subjects that the information is needed only for research purposes. It took 15 minutes to subjects to respond the scale.

The composite score of the scale was determined by adding, the corresponding scores against only one box marked on the items – 1, 2, 3, 4, 5, 6, 7, 8, 9, 10 and 11 and corresponding scores against each sub item marked under item 12 and 13.

Statistical Design:

After the scoring of personality, N-Ach and SES tests was completed, the data was subjected to statistical analysis by employing 't' test in order to get an understanding of specific personality dimensions. N-Ach and SES of both Gifted Achievers and Underachievers. Factor analysis was computed in order to determine the specific constellation of factors in gifted Achievers and Underachievers. Line graphs, Pi-charts and Bar diagrams were used in order to make the results transparent. All the statistical information is presented in the next chapter.

4

Statistical Analysis

To create satisfaction out of another's dissatisfaction is a sin.

Mahmood

In order to make a proper statistical analysis in the present study and reach the logical conclusions, the investigator has sought the expert opinion of different statisticians and educationists in the NCERT, Chandigarh University and Jammu University. Their expert opinion was substantiated by going through the books on statistics Garrett (1981), Guilford (1965), Guilford (1954), Fruchter (1967) and accordingly the following statistical techniques were finalized for the proposed study:

I. For the comparison between Gifted Achievers and Underachievers on all the 14 personality factors, Fisher's and student's `t' was employed. The information is presented in Table 08.

II. For the comparison between gifted Achievers and Underachievers on six N-Ach. factors and composite score of N-Ach. Fisher's and Student's `t' was employed. The information is cited in Table 09.

III. For the comparison of gifted Achievers and under-Achievers on SES, again Fisher's and Student's `t' was used, as shown in Table 10.

IV. Inter-correlations of 21 variables was done separately for gifted Achievers group table 12 and gifted Underachievers group Table 24.

V. The principal component method, Hotelling (1933), with varimax rotation, Kaiser (1958), was employed to find out the factor pattern associated with gifted Achievers and Underachievers. Nine factors, with eigen values of 1.00 or greater were extracted, which together accounted for 64.5% of total variance in the gifted Achievers group and 65% of total variance in the gifted Underachievers group as shown in Table 14 and Table 26 respectively. Nine factors extracted from gifted Achievers group are presented in Tables 15 to 23. And nine factors extracted in gifted under-Achievers group are cited in Tables 27 to 35. The method of Factor analysis selected for the present study has been successfully employed by (Malik, 1991; Chaudry, 1989 and Singh and Vanvaria, 1980). For the interpretation of the factors a loading of 0.30 or above for a particular variable was considered. The criterion has been fixed in line with the concept of Harman (1976) and Fruchter (1967).

VI. For an immediate understanding of the comparisons of gifted Achievers and Underachievers, on personality factors need achievement and SES, the results have been plotted in Figures 1 to 6.

The results have been analyzed in the following tables and figures:-

Table 08: Significance of mean difference between gifted Achievers (N=128) and Underachievers (N=100) on 14 Factors of HSPQ.

Personality Factors			Gifted	$\bar{x}$	S.D.	SED	't' value
	'A'						
Reserved		Warm Hearted	Achievers	9.97	5.52		
	Vs					0.33	N.S. 0.30
Aloof		Outgoing	Under Achievers	9.87	2.48		
	'B'						
Dull		Bright	Achievers	5.37	1.76		
	Vs					0.23	N.S. 1.43
Low intelligence		High intelligence	Under Achievers	5.04	1.69		
	'C'						
Emotionally less stable		Emotion-ally stable	Achievers	13.23	2.99		
	Vs					0.39	N.S. 1.85
Ego-weakness		High Ego-strength	Under Achievers	12.51	2.89		
	'D'						
Undemonstrative		Exitable	Achievers	11.43	3.31		
	Vs					0.38	N.S. 0.24
Inactive		Over-active	Under Achievers	11.34	2.58		
	'E'						
Submissive		Dominant	Achievers	8.14	2.77		
	Vs					0.39	N.S. 1.08
Obedient		Aggressive	Under Achievers	8.56	3.08		

	'F'						
Desurgency		Sugency	Achievers	10.44	3.24		
	Vs					0.4	N.S. 1.38
Serious		Happy-go lucky	Under Achievers	10.99	2.85		
	'G'						
Low super-ego strength		High super-ego strength	Achievers	13.73	3.30		
	Vs					0.44	4.61**
Disregards rules		Sense of Cuty	Under Achievers	11.70	3.31		
	'H'						
Shy		Adventu-rous	Achievers	11.12	3.21		
	Vs					0.43	N.S. 1.25
Threat Sensitive		Socially bold	Under Achievers	10.58	3.23		
	'I'						
Tough minded		Tender minded	Achievers	10.42	2.89		
	Vs					0.35	N.S. 0.37
Expects little		Sensitive	Under Achievers	10.34	2.39		
	'J'						
Liking group action		Internally restrained	Achievers	9.89	2.62		
	Vs					0.36	N.S. 0.63
Accepts common standards		Reflective	Under Achievers	9.66	2.79		
	'O'						
Untroubled		Guilt proneness	Achievers	7.44	3.29		
	Vs					0.46	2.61**
Self accured		Worriying	Under Achievers	8.64	2.92		

Q2						
Group dependent	Self sufficient	Achievers	10.10	2.83		
Vs					0.38	N.S. 1.32
Sound follower	Prefers own decisions	Under Achievers	9.98	2.86		
Q3						
Un-controlled	Contro-lled	Achievers	12.87	3.05		
Vs					0.40	N.S. 1.50
Follows own urge	Follows self image	Under Achievers	12.27	3.02		
Q4						
Low ergic tension	High ergic Tension	Achievers	9.21	3.03		
Vs					0.41	N.S. 0.64
Relaxed	Tense	Under Achievers	8.95	3.14		

Note: N.S. = Not significant
** = Probability less than 0.01.

Table 09: Significance of mean difference between gifted Achievers (N=128) and Underachievers (N=100) on 06 Factors and composite score of need - achievement.

Need Achievement Factor	Gifted	$\bar{x}$	S.D.	SED	't' value
	Achievers	2.10	1.63		
A. Hope of Success				0.20	6.15**
	Under-Achievers	0.87	1.40		
	Achievers	12.66	4.58		
B. High Ego Ideal				0.69	2.94**
	Under-Achievers	10.63	5.68		

	Achievers	2.10	1.63		
C. Perseverance				0.20	6.15**
	Under-Achievers	0.87	1.40		
	Achievers	18.97	5.75		
D. Realistic Attitude				0.77	7.78**
	Under-Achievers	12.98	5.85		
	Achievers	2.08	1.36		
E. Internal control of Fate				0.20	2.0*
	Under-Achievers	1.68	1.64		
	Achievers	0.91	0.29		
G. Incomplete				0.03	2.66**
	Under-Achievers	0.99	0.10		
	Achievers	41.73	7.58		
Composite Score of Need Achievement				1.21	9.03**
	Under-Achievers	30.80	10.11		

Note: ** = Probability less than 0.01
* = Probability less than 0.05

Table 10: Significance of Mean difference between Gifted- Achievers (N=128) and Underachievers (N=100) on Socio-Economic Status.

Gifted	$\bar{x}$	S.D.	SED	't' value
Achievers	34.91	7.68		
			1.03	2.32*
Under-Achievers	32.52	7.8		

Note * = P<0.05

Table 11: List of Variables

S. No.	Variables	Factor	Name of the variable
1.	V2	Factor A	Reserved vs Warmhearted
2	V3	Factor B	Dull vs Bright.
3.	V4	Factor C	3. Emotionally less stable vs Emotionally stable
4.	V5	Factor D	Undemonstrative vs. Excitable
5.	V6	Factor E	Obedient vs Aggressive
6.	V7	Factor F	Serious vs Happy-go-Lucky
7.	V8	Factor G	Low Super-ego strength vs. High super-ego strength
8.	V9	Factor H	Shy vs Adventurous
9.	V10	Factor I	Tough minded vs Tender minded
10.	V11	Factor J	Likes group action vs Internally restrained
11.	V12	Factor O	Untroubled vs Guilt proneness
12.	V13	Factor Q2	Sound follower vs prefers own decisions
13.	V14	Q3	Uncontrolled vs. controlled
14.	V15	Q4	Relaxed vs Tense
15.	V16	A	Hope of success
16.	V17	B	High ego ideal
17.	V18	C	Perserverance
18.	V19	D	Realistic Attitude
19.	V20	E	Internal control of fate
20.	V21	G	Incomplete
21.	V23		Socio-economic Status

Table 12: Original correlation matrix (21x21) Gifted Achievers Group (N=128)

	V2	V3	V4	V5	V6	V7	V8
V23	0706	0163	0201	-0429	0260	0526	-0385
V21	0909	-0771	-1024	-0372	2099*	0548	-1412
V20	-0509	1357	0659	0393	0644	0143	-0031
V19	-0332	2223	0133	-0881	-0900	0413	2945*
V18	-1149	0449	0933	0456	0340	-0690	1188
V17	0616	1877*	0977	0898	-0846	-1234	1947*
V16	-0739	1570	0344	-0473	0096	0794	1440
V15	0529	0788	-0851	0606	-0437	-1197	-0288
V14	-1428	2588**	2725**	-0795	-1042	0892	2887**
V13	-0419	0995	0644	1077	1021	0304	1114
V12	-0174	-1926	-2608**	-0690	1370	0234	2386**
V11	0354	0337	-0085	0757	-0333	-0253	0231
V10	0929	-1961*	0242	0267	-0603	0557	0048
V9	0179	2029*	1099	0258	-2788**	0914	2062*
V8	-0969	2949**	2633**	0702	-1975*	0178	
V7	1332	0938	0301	-0459	0097		
V6	-0002	-0892	-0387	-0449			
V5	0848	-0284	0090				
V4	0104	0791					
V3	-0637						
V2							

-0373	-1183	-0300	0701	-0468	-0124	0293	0799	0255
-1434	0319	0087	1621	0807	-0159	0887	-1692*	-0888
-0546	-0529	1310	0728	0439	0775	-0325	0534	1601
0724	-0292	1724*	-2053*	0001	1326	0150	3148**	0431
0690	0263	0460	-1901*	-0224	0181	-0475	0739	1683*
1688*	-0081	-0010	-0665	-0049	1406	-0801	0241	
-0219	0361	-0231	-1611	-0516	1210	-1440		
-0029	0059	1249	1621	1223	-1626			
1968	0225	-0172	-1655	-0127				
0619	-0748	-0853	-0294					
-0403	-0673	0070						
-0749	0848							
0031								
V9	V10	V11	V12	V13	V14	V15	V16	V17

-0117	1326	0358	-0300	
-3275 **	-0743	-1038		
1170	0338			
1595				
V18	V19	V20	V21	V23

* Probability (0.05 level)
** Probability (0.01 level)

Note: Decimal points omitted

Table 13: Varimax rotated factor Gifted Achiever Group (N=128)

	1	2	3	4	5	6	7	8	9	h_2(comm-unality)
V2	-37715*	34695*	09999	-42452*	08460	08344	26703	01884	15646	56309
V3	34175*	-00825	42162	37950*	28835	09419	24701	13560	11141	62248
V4	64834*	-09975	-04749	-18245	-14146	02292	08800	-13926	07850	51967
V5	-03930	-01585	01127	-06191	02170	-07677	-04064	-04749	85163*	74130
V6	02436	03427	-01179	14809	-75503*	20754	15537	-09950	09394	67984
V7	08746	02032	-00726	-03818	-02739	12520	80676*	10483	-01889	68821
V8	63392*	06858	16009	27411	28116	-00719	01784	-13870	15095	62877
V9	15788	-18849	-14478	09223	63645*	25699	22939	-15668	-18798	67355
V10	12526	04320	01022	-66764*	07466	-02363	03327	-18905	08425	51349
V11	00610	-04321	-05593	-03158	06332	-83275*	-06642	-03832	07757	71541
V12	-27285	17991	-61150*	28110	-05308	-05158	18270	03820	-21170	64490
V13	14490	19314	-00880	48142*	-02417	32005*	07943	-38719*	38203*	69533
V14	78863*	06276	02470	-06494	05361	03944	-03736	09401	-15457	66926
V15	-29318	23138	-17697	37427*	33497*	25173	-11778	-23346	07963	56118
V16	-03737	-17888	55157*	-05970	-23116	14539	09952	11701	01616	43961
V17	13352	-16430	10709	02005	03105	50962*	-60000*	17821	04328	71100
V18	-02253	-75393*	09951	07358	-08192	-02022	-06765	-19256	-04201	63475
V19	-09898	05449	65366*	25730	05867	-33662*	04996	-06179	-31628*	72935
V20	10087	-34706*	-31151*	19220	-21552	-24483	16271	46238*	33087	72074
V21	-00897	73745*	-13714	09891	-29509	-03556	02550	-12357	-07932	-68305
V23	-09710	15066	09689	12467	02820	13462	02643	79392*	-07911	71325

*Significant loading

Note: Decimal points omitted

Table 14: Factors alongwith their eigen value, percentage of variance and cumulative percentage (varimax) Gifted Achievers Group (N = 128)

Factor	Eigen Value	Percentage variance	Cumulative percentage
01	2.381	11.3	11.3
02	1.733	8.3	19.6
03	1.676	7.9	27.5
04	1.559	7.4	34.9
05	1.463	7.0	41.9
06	1.326	6.3	48.2
07	1.215	5.8	54.0
08	1.160	5.5	59.5
09	1.047	5.0	64.5

Table 15: Factor – 01A "Adjustment VARIMAX ROTATED FACTOR –01A

Variable No.	Name of the variable	Loading
V14	Uncontrolled vs. controlled	.78863
V4	Emotionally less stable vs. Emotionally stable	.64834
V8	Low super-ego strength vs. High super-ego strength	.63392
V3	Dull vs. Bright	.34175
V2	Reserved vs Warmhearted	.37715

Table 16: Factor – 02A "Satisfaction vs.Dissatsifaction VARIMAX ROTATED FACTOR –02A

Variable No.	Name of the variable	Loading
V21	Incomplete	.73745
V2	Reserved vs Warmhearted	.34695
V18	Perserverance	-.75393
V20	Internal control of fate	-.34706

Table 17: Factor – 03A "Optimism" VARIMAX ROTATED FACTOR –03A		
Variable No.	**Name of the variable**	**Loading**
V19	Realistic attitude	.65366
V2	Hope of success	.55157
V3	Dull vs. Bright	.42162
V12	Untroubled vs. Guilt proneness	-.61150
V20	Internal control of Fate	-.31151

Table 18: Factor – 04A "Self-Reliant-cum-Apprehensive" VARIMAX ROTATED FACTOR –04A		
Variable No.	**Name of the variable**	**Loading**
V13	Sound Follower vs Prefers own decisions	.48142
V32	Dull vs Bright	.37950
V15	Relaxed vs tense	.37427
V10	Tough minded vs. Tender minded	-.66764
V2	Reserved vs warmhearted	-.42452

Table 19: Factor – 05A "Adventurous-cum-Sensitive" VARIMAX ROTATED FACTOR –05A		
Variable No.	**Name of the variable**	**Loading**
V9	Shy vs Adventurous	.63645
V15	Relaxed vs Tense	.33497
V6	Obedient vs Aggressive	-.75503

Table 20: Factor – 06A "High level of Aspiration-cum-group dependent" VARIMAX ROTATED FACTOR –06A		
Variable No.	**Name of the variable**	**Loading**
V17	High Ego-Ideal	.50962
V13	Sound follower vs prefers own decisions	.32005
V11	Likes group action vs Internally restrained	-.83275
V19	Realistic Attitude	-.33662

Table 21: Factor – 07A "Calm vs Enthusiastic" VARIMAX ROTATED FACTOR –07A		
Variable No.	**Name of the variable**	**Loading**
V7	Serious vs. Happy-go-Lucky	.80676
V17	High ego-ideal	-.60000

Table 22: Factor – 08A "Social status-cum-Self-determination" VARIMAX ROTATED FACTOR –08A		
Variable No.	**Name of the variable**	**Loading**
V23	Socio-economic status	.79392
V20	Internal control of fate	.46238
V13	Sound follower vs prefers own decisions	-.38719

Table 23: Factor – 09A "Excitable-cum-Committed" VARIMAX ROTATED FACTOR –09A		
Variable No.	**Name of the variable**	**Loading**
V5	Undemonstrative vs Excitable	.85163
V13	Sound followers vs prefers own decision	.38203
V20	Internal control of fate	.33087
V19	Realistic attitude	-.31628

Table 24: Inter-Correlation Matrix (21x21), Gifted underachievers Group (N=100)

	V2	V3	V4	V5	V6	V7	V8	V9	V10	V11	V12	V13	V14	V15	V16	V17	V18	V19	V20	V21	V23
V2		-0625	0110	0848	-0002	1332	-0969	0179	0929	0365	-0174	-0419	-1428	0529	-0739	-0616	-1149	-0332	-0509	0909	0696
V3			0791	-0284	-0892	0938	2949**	2029*	-1961*	0337	-1926	0995	2508**	0788	1570	1877*	0449	2223	1357	-0771	-0163
V4				0090	-0387	0301	2633**	1099	0242	-0085	-2608**	0644	2725**	-0851	0344	0977	0933	0133	0659	-1024	0201
V5					-0450	-0459	0702	0258	0267	0757	-0690	1077	-0795	0606	-0473	0898	0456	-0881	0393	-0372	-0429
V6						0086	-1975*	-2788**	-0703	-0333	1370	1021	-1242	-0437	0096	-0846	0340	-0920	0644	2099*	0260
V7							0178	0914	0557	-0253	0234	0304	0892	-1117	0794	-1234	-0690	0413	0143	0548	0416
V8								2062*	0037	0231	2375**	1114	2887**	-0277	1440	1947*	1176	2945**	-0031	-1412	-0385

V9	V10	V11	V12	V13	V14	V15	V16	V17
-0263	-1183	-0290	0701	-0454	-0124	0289	0787	0255
-1434	-0319	0087	1621	0807	-0159	0887	-1692 *	-0877
-0546	-0529	1310	0728	0439	0775	-0325	0534	1601
0724	-0292	1724*	-2053 *	-0007	1326	0150	3148 **	0431
0690	0263	0460	-1901 *	-0224	0181	-0475	0739	1683*
1688*	-0081	-0010	-0665	-0049	1406	-0801	0241	
-0219	0361	-0231	-1611	-0516	1210	-1439		
-0029	0059	1249	1621	1223	-1616			
1257	0225	-0172	-1655	-0127				
0619	-0748	-0853	-0283					
-0403	-0673	0070						
-0749	0837							
0023								

V18	V19	V20	V21	V23
-0117	1226	0358	-0200	
-3265 **	-0743	-1038		
1170	0335			
1585				

* Probability (0.05 level)
** Probability (0.01 level)

Note: Decimal points omitted.

Table 25: Varimax rotated factor Gifted Underachievers Group (N=100)

	1	2	3	4	5	6	7	8	9	h_2(communality)
V2	05096	-23319	00170	13513	15961	03180	78085*	-01359	08440	71875
V3	10386	22106	45369*	05090	16738	-56040*	-03058	-07577	-02300	61736
V4	26023	-05908	18421	-00681	62160*	02510	04787	02526	36868*	63106
V5	07760	-13288	-10804	72856*	-07600	-05958	08203	01303	04859	58474
V6	-76205*	-10748	05229	-02070	-09184	-03201	-01292	11468	04930	62064
V7	16007	43519*	-01070	-12508	-13259	01032	69123*	07118	-06538	73560
V8	33579*	46028*	-07534	32208*	35473*	-01725	-13423	-01980	-16220	60487
V9	72307*	-02759	09812	14179	46383*	-06988	19553	09564	-00225	60966
V10	04557	09859	-01909	-01761	-05322	87378*	04485	-11047	11970	80823
V11	-33405*	30208*	30952*	20569	18791	19063	25131	-18405	29464	57195
V12	-01242	-12319	16401	05822	-81370	11592	-07670	-11338	30291*	83166
V13	-18409	-06864	12845	-03183	15419	00846	15031	76671*	02235	69091
V14	40283*	23916	33423*	-35961*	24683	-10049	09072	-13323	06197	56133
V15	-14546	-26318	06458	01723	08812	50767*	-03594	16662	34530*	50867
V16	00459	68304*	-06202	-31510*	-08055	-01841	02570	01697	-04092	57915
V17	21794	02653	56809*	52843*	07625	12797	-02561	-23899	-02133	73058
V18	00482	25740	20111	45583	11619	18347	-16343	34609*	-09482	51715
V19	04460	69620*	14265	10090	12558	-08670	02291	-03707	15137	56531
V20	-05936	-01376	80088*	11841	-11263	-02310	00254	-16902	-10460	71188
V21	-37100*	-02987	17493	-10468	12151	06493	18620	-60739*	-22508	65333
V23	-04488	10174	-13787	-01101	-08684	-02980	04123	09115	86200*	79298

*Signiricant loading

Note: Decimal points omitted.

Table 26:	**Factors alongwith their eigen value, percentage of variacne and cumulative percentage (varimax) gifted Underachievers Group (n=100)**		
Factors	**Eigen value**	**Percentage variance**	**Cumulative percentage**
01	2.787	13.3	13.3
02	1.743	8.3	21.6
03	1.608	7.7	29.3
04	1.539	7.3	36.6
05	1.384	6.6	43.2
06	1.252	6.0	49.2
07	1.219	5.8	55.0
08	1.077	5.1	60.1
09	1.034	4.9	65.0

Table 27: Factor – 01U "Extroversion vs. Introversion VARIMAX ROTATED FACTOR –01U		
Variable No.	**Name of the variable**	**Loading**
V9	Shy vs. Adventurous	.72307
V14	Uncontrolled vs. controlled	.40283
V8	Low super ego strength High super ego strength	.33579
V6	Obedient vs. Aggressive	-.76205
V21	Incomplete	-.37100
V11	Likes group action vs. Internally restrained	-.33405

Table 28: Factor – 02U "Aspirant-cum-happy-go-lucky" VARIMAX ROTATED FACTOR –02U		
Variable No.	**Name of the variable**	**Loading**
V19	Realistic attitude	.69620
V16	Hope of success	.68304
V8	Low super ego strength vs high super-ego strength	.46028
V7	Serious vs happy-go-lucky	.43519
V11	Likes group action vs internally restrained	.30208

Table 29: Factor – 03U"Pragmatic-cum-individualistic" VARIMAX ROTATED FACTOR –-3U		
Variable No.	**Name of the variable**	**Loading**
V20	Internal control of fate	.80088
V17	High ego-ideal	.56809
V3	Dull vs. Bright	.45369
V14	Uncontrolled vs controlled	.33423
V11	Likes group action vs Internally restrained	.30952

Table 30: Factor – 04U"Excitable-cum-Egoistic" VARIMAX ROTATED FACTOR –04U		
Variable No.	**Name of the variable**	**Loading**
V5	Undemonstrative vs. Excitable	.72858
V17	High Ego-Ideal	.52843
V18	Perserverance	.45583
V8	Low super ego strength vs High super-ego strength	.32208
V14	Uncontrolled vs controlled	.-35961
V16	Hope of success	-.31510

Table 31: Factor – 05U"Placid-cum-Adventurous" VARIMAX ROTATED FACTOR –05U		
Variable No.	**Name of the variable**	**Loading**
V4	Emotionally less stable vs Emotionally stable	.62160
V9	Shy vs Adventurous	.46383
V8	Low super-ego strength vs High super ego strength	.35473
V12	Untroubled vs. Guilt proness	-81.1370

Table 32: Factor – 06U"Sensitive-cum-Tense" VARIMAX ROTATED FACTOR –06U		
Variable No.	**Name of the variable**	**Loading**
V10	Tough minded vs Tender minded	.87378
V15	Relaxed vs Tense	.50767
V3	Dull vs Bright	-.56040

Table 33: Factor – 07U"Sociability" VARIMAX ROTATED FACTOR –07U		
Variable No.	**Name of the variable**	**Loading**
V2	Reserved vs Warmhearted	.78085
V7	Serious vs Happy go lucky	.69123

Table 34: Factor – 08U "Decisive" VARIMAX ROTATED FACTOR –08U		
Variable No.	**Name of the variable**	**Loading**
V13	Sound follower vs prefers own decision	.76671
V18	Perserverance	.34609
V21	Incomplete	-.60739

Table 35: Factor – 09U "Pragmatic-cum-Individualistic" VARIMAX ROTATED FACTOR –09U		
Variable No.	**Name of the variable**	**Loading**
V23	Socio-economic status	.86200
V4	Emotionally less stable vs Emotionally stable	.36868
V15	Relaxed vs Tense	.34530
V12	Untroubled vs Guilt proness	.30291

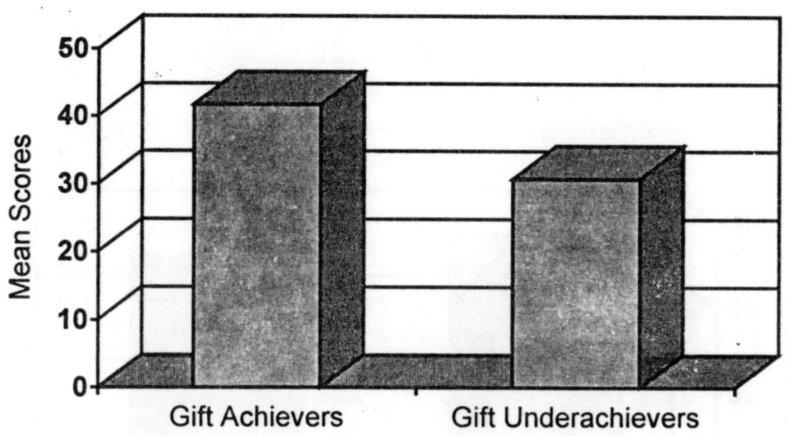

Figure 3: Comparison between Gifted Achievers (N = 128) and Underachievers (N=100) on Composite score of Need Achievement.

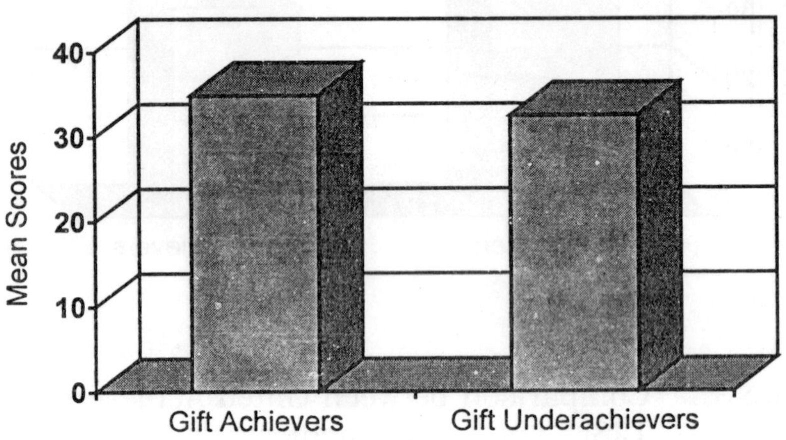

Figure 4: Comparison between Gifted Achievers (N = 128) and Underachievers (N=100) on Socio-Economic Status.

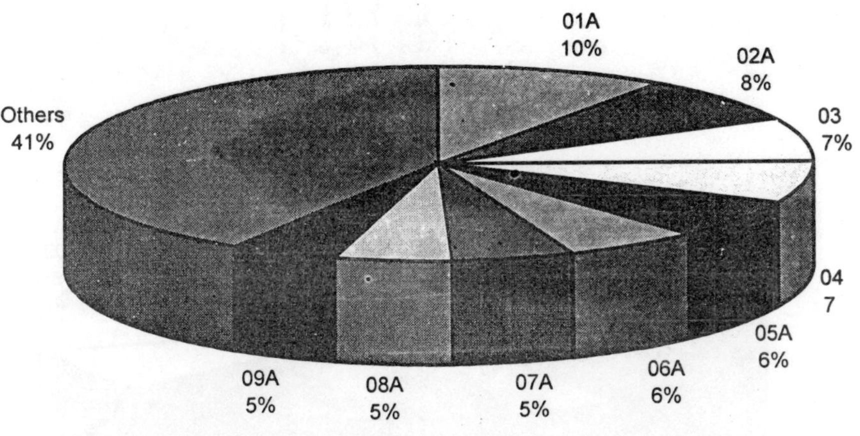

Figure 5: Factor-wise percentage of variance Gifted Achievers Group (N=128)

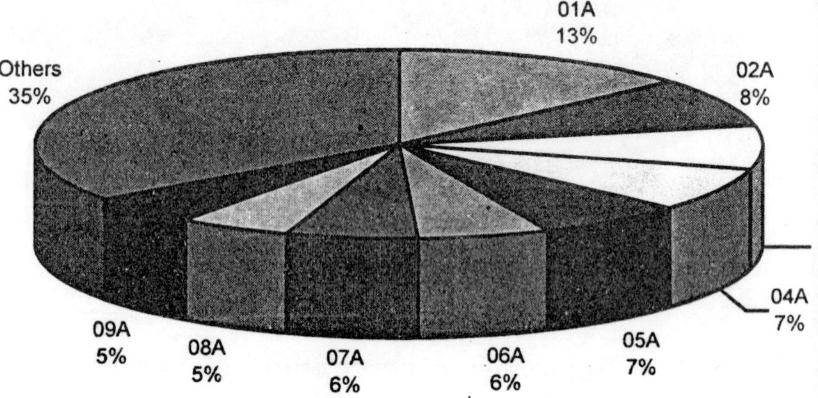

Figure 6: Factor-wise percentage of variance Gifted Underachievers Group (N=100)

The pooled information in the above cited tables and figures got through the appropriate statistical techniques employed, has been summed up and discussed in the next chapter.

Discussion and Interpretation

If affection is sacred peace reigns.

Mahmood

Education and psychology are two important aspects which shape the personality characteristics of young boys and girls. Obviously it becomes imperative for parents, teachers and researchers that an objective cause and effect relationship is built up while looking for various factors which make teaching and learning effective and purposive. Most of the researchers, working on scholastic achievement, level of Intelligence vis-a-vis other personality characteristics, establish different types of associations with these factors. In the present study a modest attempt has been made to find out the factors which interfere or go with the normal scholastic achievement of the gifted children. Accordingly a number of factors, viz. personality profiles, need achievement and socio-economic status, included in the present investigation, were screened and on the basis of the analysis of data the findings which have surfaced are being discussed in the present chapter.

Personality profiles:

For the measurement of personality profiles Cattelles 14 HSPQ, Urdu adaptation, by the present investigator, was employed and the findings as shown in Table - 08 and Fig.-1 are discussed as under:-

Table 08 makes it obvious that the mean of gifted Achievers (9.97) is superior to gifted Underachievers mean (9.87) on factor 'A' of HSPQ. It seems, therefore, that gifted Achievers are warmhearted and outgoing whereas Underachievers are reserved and aloof. But as the mean difference is not statistically significant no decision can be taken. However, the norm Table depicts that by converting the means of both the groups on factor "A" into stens, they fall into the average group. Therefore, both the groups are neither warm-hearted or outgoing nor reserved or aloof. As such the groups do not differ from each other on this factor.

The mean of gifted Achievers (5.37) incomparison to gifted Underachievers (5.07) on factor "B" of HSPQ is slightly higher but statistically it is not significant. Besides HSPQ measures crystallized intelligence, as in the traditional tests, rather than fluid intelligence, as in the culture fair tests (Cattell, 1963). Gifted Achievers may be faster on crystallized ability which may be a function of their greater attention to school achievement. Therefore, the results that gifted Achievers do not differ from gifted Underachievers on I.Q. is justified.

The mean of gifted Achievers (13.23) is higher than the mean of gifted Underachievers (12.55) on factor "C" of HSPQ. It can be inferred therefore, that gifted Achievers are emotionally stable and possess high ego-strength whereas gifted Underachievers are emotionally instable and have ego-weakness. The mean difference is significant at. 07 level but not at .05 level. Therefore though the probability is less than 7% no conclusive decision can be taken. While comparing the results with the norm table both the groups fall in the emotionally stable category.

On factor "D" (undemonstrative or Inactive vs excitable and impatient) both the groups show a slight mean difference (.09) which is not statistically significant. Therefore, the two groups do not differ on this factor. By converting the means of both the groups into stens the norm table depicts that both gifted Achievers and Underachievers can be termed as excitable and overactive, as both the groups have a sten value of 06. It is, however, commonsense that as both the groups are gifted, their intellectual potential would not allow them to be undemonstrative or inactive. They have to give expression to their intellectual potential in any manner - academic or non-academic.

The perusal of the table 08 makes it evident that the mean of gifted Underachievers (8.56) is higher than gifted Achievers (8.14) on factor 'E' of HSPQ. It seems that gifted Underachievers are dominant and aggressive in-comparison to gifted Achievers who tend to be submissive and obedient but as the mean difference is not significant statistically at .05 level, therefore, nothing with precision can be accepted. However, when the means are examined from the point of view of the sten values, the norm table (HSPQ) makes it clear that the means of both the groups fall in the average category. Thus, both the groups are neither highly dominant or aggressive nor highly submissive or obedient.

On factor "F" of HSPQ there is a mean difference of 0.55 between gifted Achievers and Underachievers and it seems that gifted Achievers are serious and desurgent whileas gifted Underachievers are happy-go-luckly and surgent. But the results are not significant statistically even at .05 level. Therefore, empirically, it is to be accepted that the two groups do not differ from each other on this factor. When the means of both the groups were converted into sten scores it is ascertained that both gifted Achievers and Underachievers are neither more surgent or happy-go-luckily nor more desurgent or serious. Both the groups belong to the average category. Therefore, the insignificance of results on this factor is more strengthened.

From the perusal of the table 08 it is established that the means of gifted Achievers and Underachievers differ significantly from each other (p.01) on factor "G". Therefore, it can be safely concluded that gifted Achievers have high super-ego strength, sense of duty, determination, perseverance and they are responsible, emotionally disciplined, consistently ordered, concerned about moral standards and rules. On the other hand, gifted Underachievers are possessing low super-ego strength, disregard rules; are fickle, self indulgent, undependable and disregard obligations to people. Therefore. gifted Achievers have a tendency to drive the ego and to restrain the Id, Underachievers have weak super-ego strength and thus fall prey to oscillation and weak organization of thinking. It is only when a student has a sense of duty that he tries his level best to do his assignment and home work assigned by the concerned teacher on an appropriate time. Obviously he will be a good achiever. On the other hand the other student, who disregards rules and has no sense of duty, does not complete his home work (assigned by the concerned teacher) in time, which results into his under-achievement.

So far as the results on factor "H" (Shy vs adventurous) are concerned the mean of gifted Achievers is higher than the mean of gifted Underachievers. This mean difference shows that the gifted Achievers are adventurous or socially bold and gifted Underachievers are shy and threat-sensitive. But the obtained 't' value (1.25) is far less than the table 't' value (1.97) at .05 level.

Therefore, no decision can be taken. However, the norm table HSPQ depicts that the mean of both the groups on the said factor is above average i.e. H+. The statistical insignificance of the results is further substantiated because both the groups have 07 as sten value. Thus it can be inferred from the results that gifted Achievers and under-achieveers do not differ significantly on this factor. And both the groups have a tendency to be adventurous in comparison to the population. As both the groups are gifted it is obvious that the groups are adventurous also.

The perusal of the table 08 makes it evident that gifted Achievers differ slightly from gifted Underachievers on factor "I" (Tough minded vs Tender minded). The obtained 't' value 0.37 is extremely lower than table 't' value at 0.05 level (1.97). Thus the groups do not differ from each other on this factor. The norm table makes it obvious that the sten score for both the means is 06 on the said factor. I+ depicts that both the groups are tender-minded and sensitive in comparison to the population. Both the groups being gifted can not be spectators at any instance.

On factor 'J' (liking group action vs Internally restrained) the mean difference is very low and statistically not significant. Therefore, gifted Achievers do not differ from gifted Underachievers on this factor. The perusal of the norm table depicts that the mean of both the groups falls on the sten score of 07. Therefore, both the groups are reflective, internally restrained in comparison to the population and fall into the J+ category. Cattell (1976) observes that individuals prefer to do things on their own. They are Intellectually and physically fastidious, think-over their mistakes and how to avoid them, tend not to forget if they are unfairly treated, have private views differing from the group. The results in the present investigation are justified from the point of view of Cattell. As gifted Achievers and

Underachievers in the present study belong to the intellectually superior category, they do not differ on this factor. They have their own decisions in order to deal with any situation, because of intellectual superiority.

So far as the Factor 'O' is concerned, the mean of Gifted Achievers (7.44) is less than the mean of Gifted Underachievers (8.64) and statistically significant (p<.01). It indicates that Gifted Achievers are untroubled, self assured, serene, self-confident, insensitive to people's approval or disapproval and have no fears; whereas Gifted Underachievers exhibit guilt proneness tendencies, are worrying, insecure, self reproaching, cry easily, insecure, sensitive to people's obligations and disapproval, have loneliness and brooding tendencies. The results appeal to logic that it is only as the Gifted Achievers are confident, self assured and untroubled that they achieve to the level of their potential. Gifted Underachievers do not achieve to the level of their expected achievement because they are possessing guilt proneness, worrying, loneliness and insecurity characteristic. Catteil (1976) observes that O+ persons have a sense of inferiority and inadequacy in meeting the rough daily demands of life. Besides, Cattell (1957) and king (1948) hold that in O+ scorers definite fears as well as central feeling of inadequacy and loneliness are prominent. As a matter of fact, even for a layman, the inference becomes obvious that as Gifted Underachievers fall in the O+ category their underachievement is but necessary.

On Factor Q2 the Gifted Achievers and Underachievers have a slight mean difference (.03), with an obtained 't' value of 0.32 which is far beyond the table value at 0.05 level. Therefore, the two groups do not differ significantly on this factor (Self-sufficient vs group dependent). The sten value of both the means is '05' which is an average mean. Therefore, both the groups are neither group dependent nor self-sufficient. They possess the average of both.

The mean score of Gifted Achievers (12.87) is superior to the mean score of Gifted Underachievers (12.27) on Factor Q3. The obtained 't' value is, no doubt, as high as 1.50 but has not reached to the level of significance as the table 't' value with 226 df is 1.97. Therefore, it can be said with certainty that the two groups do not differ significantly from each other on this factor (uncontrolled vs controlled). A look at the norm table makes it clear that the mean of both the groups falls in the average category (sten value 06). But as the direction is towards +side, both the groups possess Q3+ characteristics in comparison to the general population. Thus both the groups, Gifted Achievers and Underachievers, are controlled by and follow self-image. As both the groups possess high intellectual potential, they understand the delicacy of every thing in shorter duration of time and react, taking into account their own self-image.

The perusal of table on Q4 (low ergic-tension vs High ergic-tension) makes it evident that Gifted Achievers and Underachievers differ very slightly on this factor. The mean difference is not statistically significant ($p>.05$). obtained 't' value is 0.63, this is far below the table 't' value at .05 level (1.97). Therefore, it can be ascertained that both the groups have the same standing on this factor. The norm table depicts that the mean of both the groups falls in between (sten 06). Therefore, both the groups have the direction towards +side. Both the groups seem to have a bit of inclination to be tense in comparison to the population. It appeals to the logic also that Gifted (whether Achiever or underachiever) possess a sharp eye. Whatever they observe, they observe with critical understanding. Therefore, it may result into their being tense when compared to their peers.

The results of the present study depicted in table 08 are further substantiated by Fig.1. There is an obvious difference between gifted Achievers and underchievers on personality factors C,G,O and Q3. But the differences are statistically significant only on factors G and O as discussed already.

The results of table 08 and Fig.1, discussed and analysed above, are in line with Terman and Oden (1947), Morgan (1952), Roe (1952), Durr and collier (1960), Bledshoe and Garrison (1962), Taylor (1964), Purkey (1969), Whitemore (1980), Sternberg (1985). Terman and Oden(1947) have found that gifted Underachievers lack self-confidence, have an inability to persevere and possess inferiority feelings. Morgan (1952) on a study of high ability Achievers and Underachievers concluded that achievement of high ability Achievers is associated with maturity and seriousness of interest, persuasiveness and self-confidence. Roe (1952) has found that all the 64 scientists had in common a driving absorption in their work. They worked for long hours for many years, frequently no vacations to speak of because they would prefer to do their work than anything else. Durr and collier (1960) have found that low achieving gifted students exhibit withdrawal tendencies, lack of self-confidence, self-reliance and a sense of personal freedom. Bledshoe and Garrison (1962) have indicated that high Achievers, especially the gifted, were found to be self-confident and assertive in facing new and difficult tasks. They were functioning intellectually in an active and independent manner, whereas Underachievers withdrew into daydreams or unreachable passivity and were defensive in order to maintain their integrity. Taylor (1964) has made it evident that overAchievers are self-confident and optimistic whereas Underachievers possess feelings of inadequacy and withdrawal in attempting to be self-sufficient. Purkey (1969) has made it clear that lack of perseverance and inadequate expression contribute to underachievement among the Gifted students. While summing up some of the most important traits of gifted Underachievers Whitemore (1980) has highlighted lack of concentration as a characteristic feature of gifted Underachievers. Sternberg (1986) has found that personality characteristics which hinder gifted Underachievers progress are - lack of persistence or perseverance; failure to initiate; excessive self-pity and feeling sorry for one self; excessive dependence or over reliance on other.

The results are partly in line with Mufson, et al (1989) who have found that in comparison to bright Achievers Underachievers are less confident, less emotionally and socially mature, less able to focus on one concern at a time, less accurate in their perception about themselves and their work. Kulshrestha (1981) has revealed in her study that bright Underachievers in Mathematics are more warmhearted than normal Achievers and bright normal Achievers in English are more conscientious than bright Underachievers. Mennon (1972) made it clear in her study that over achieving group of superior boys and girls are less extrovert,less maladjusted than Underachievers and show greater academic interest and endurance. Havinghurst (1961) and Gowan (1955) are of the opinion that gifted achieving students are better adjusted emotionally than the non-achieving students. Though in the present study also the Gifted Achievers are shown emotionally more stable than Gifted Underachievers ($p<.07$) yet it has not achieved the significance level of ($p<.05$). Therefore, no conclusive decision about emotional stability or Instability can be taken. However, the results being in the same track can not be overlooked outright. Keeping in view the results on all the 14 factors of HSPQ, the hypothesis number 01,

"Gifted Achievers and Underachievers differ significantly so far as their personality factors are concerned", is partly acceptable.

Need Achievement:

For the measurement of need Achievement Urdu adaptation of Mukherjee's Incomplete sentences Blank by the present author was used and the results shown in table-09 and Fig. 2 and 3 are discussed as under:

The perusal of table 09 makes it obvious that Gifted Achievers and Underachievers differ significantly on Factor 'A' (Hope of success) of Need Achievement (N Ach). The obtained 't' value is 6.15 which is far greater than table 't' value at 01 level. The mean difference favours Gifted Achievers. Indicating thereby that gifted Achievers are high on Hope of success than gifted Underachievers. The results support the contention that gifted Achievers achieve because they are optimistic. Whatever task they are assigned they complete. They Identify themselves with a successful authority and follow his ideals. Besides, they prefer intrinsic rewards when successful, that gives them boosting for further action. On the other hand gifted Underachievers underachieve because they have fear of failure. They are pessimistic about their success. It provides a negative feed-back for the gifted Underachievers and they fail to realize their potentiality. They hardly identify themselves with any successful authority that would have provided a motivating force for their success. They usually prefer external rewards for their success. The denial of such rewards becomes a negative force against the struggle for achievement. The results are in the expected direction that gifted Achievers possess hope of success while gifted Underachievers have fear of failure.

On Factor 'B' (Ego-ideal) the table depicts that the mean of gifted Achievers (12.66) is decidedly superior to the mean of gifted Underachievers (10.63). The mean difference is significant beyond 01% ($P<.01$) level. The results confirm that gifted Achievers have high Ego-ideal than gifted Underachievers. Gifted Achievers possess high level of aspiration and that is why they achieve success. They have high level of self-confidence. Besides this they have a sense of striving to achieve a high position or status in society and therefore, strive for achieving that status. Competitiveness and maintenance of self-respect enables them to look forward to success. On the other hand, gifted Underachievers lack self-confidence and competitiveness. With the result they fall in line with the average Achievers. They hardly have a sense of striving to achieve high status in society. Therefore, they are not endowed with the characteristics that would have served as a motivating force for achieving at least upto their inborn capability and thus prove to be Underachievers. The results of the present study show that gifted Achievers have high Ego-ideal while gifted Underachievers possess low Ego-ideal. This appeals to the logic in the sense that high Ego-ideal serves as a positive feed-back, while low Ego-ideal serves a negative feed-back for success.

The mean difference (9.22) between gifted Achievers and Underachievers on factor 'G' Perseverance is statistically significant ($p<.01$). The results confirm that gifted Achievers are persistent, prefer difficult and challenging tasks, have a sense of devotion to work, get satisfaction in completing an assigned task, have a long term involvement with future career and dislike idleness; while the reverse is true for gifted Underachievers group. The results signify that gifted Underachievers underachieve because they have less perseverance capacity and do not have more devotion to work. They usually shirk to work on difficult and challenging tasks and only work for immediate gains. As a matter of fact gifted underachievement is expected. Perseverance enables a person to achieve strides in his life. Unless a student works persistently throughout the year, he cannot get through the examination. Gifted Underachievers though pass the examination but with 2nd or 3rd division, when it is expected that their achievement should be commensurate with their intellectual potential - Ist division at least. Therefore, it is justified that gifted Achievers have high perseverance while low perseverance is the characteristic feature of gifted Underachievers.

Gifted Achievers and Underachievers differ significantly on Factor 'D' Realistic Attitude. The obtained 't' value is 7.78 which is decidedly greater than table 't' value (2.60) with 226 df. at 0.01 level. The results reveal that gifted Achievers have a realistic attitude, they take immediate risks in life, plan in advance for doing something and are able to achieve upto their optimum level. It is their realistic aspiration that they are in a position to fulfil their objectives and do not become perturbed due to failure. On the other hand gifted Underachievers have unrealistic attitude indicating thereby that they take high or low risks in their life and possess unrealistic aspirations in life. They hardly plan beforehand in order to complete a particular task. Those of the Gifted, who do not follow the sequential order-realistic aspiration, advance planning so as to perform a task, become Underachievers. On the other hand, the gifted who follow the orderly scheme prove to be Achievers. The results that gifted Achievers have realistic attitude and gifted Underachievers unrealistic also appeals to the logic in the sense that a group of subjects is named as Achievers and another termed as Underachievers.

While reviewing Table 09 it is observed that there is a significant mean difference between gifted Achievers and Underachievers on factor 'E' Internal Control of Fate of Need Achievement. The obtained 't' value on the said factor is 2.0 which is greater than table 't' value at .05 level. Therefore, the difference is statistically significant. The results confirm that gifted Achievers rely on their own effort for doing anything in life and deny the role of some superior unknown force in shaping their destiny. Strong determination is their characteristic feature. On the other hand gifted Underachievers do not rely on self effort. They are in favour of some unknown superior force in shaping their fate and have weak determination for doing any thing in life. This characteristic feature of gifted Underachievers provides itself a justification for their underachievement being natural. A person, who is not determined to do anything and does not make use of his own effort, can never realize the potential he is bestowed with. Under these circumstances he has to continue with his underachievement and prove to be an average student in the classroom. The gifted Achievers will continue to be Achievers as they rely on their own effort and work with strong determination. The results have not reached to the significance level of 0.01 because Internal control of Fate ('E' factor) factor under discussion denies the role of some superior unknown force in shaping one's destiny. And as almost all the sample subjects were believers in God, they believed that despite their hard work it is He who can bestow success on them. He shapes the fate of humanity, the human beings have only to struggle their best and energize their effort for success. Because of this faith gifted Achievers also score low on this dimension of Internal Control of Fate. Therefore, as is obvious, it affected the results on Internal control of Fate. However, the results are significant ($p<0.05$). And we can justifiably say that the gifted Achievers have high Internal control of fate than gifted Underachievers.

Factor 'G' Incomplete, as depicted on the table, shows a high mean of gifted Underachievers (0.99) while Achievers have a mean of (0.91). The mean difference is in favour of gifted Underachievers and is statistically significant ($p<0.01$). The results indicate that gifted Achievers have a tendency to leave things incomplete while gifted Achievers complete their work. The results are commensurate with the common thinking pattern in public either. It is the result of incomplete nature of home assignment, reading and writing, that a child though with gifted potential Underachieves while an average student with average I.Q. and diligence excels and achieves to the optimum level of his cognitive ability. Therefore, the results are in the expected direction.

The results, as presented in Table 09 on all the factors of Need Achievement, are further substantiated by Fig. 2. The differences between gifted Achievers and Underachievers are distinct on all the factors of Need Achievement - A, B, C, E and G. The perusal of the Fig. 02 indicates that Gifted Achievers have high Hope of Success, Ego-ideal, Perseverance, Realistic Attitude, Internal Control of Fate and Tendency to complete the assigned work while the reverse is true about Gifted Underachievers.

When Gifted Achievers and Underachievers were compared on composite score of Need Achievement the mean difference was found to be significant. The gifted Achievers had a mean score of 41.73 and Gifted Underachievers exhibited a mean Need Achievement score of 30.80. The obtained 't' value is 9.03 which is far beyond the table 't' value at 0.01 level (2.60). Therefore, it can be accepted with surety that Gifted Achievers are decidedly better than Gifted Underachievers on Need Achievement. Commonsense of a person also rationalizes one's psyche that Gifted Underachievers have very low desire to excel that is why they lag behind. And Gifted Achievers aspire more, strive for that, reach their destination and as is obvious, become Achievers.

Discussion and Interpretation

The results of table 09 on the composite score of Need Achievement have been presented in Fig. 3. The Fig. substantiates the results already discussed above that there is a remarkable difference between Gifted Achievers and Underachievers on composite score of Need Achievement. Gifted Achievers are characterized by high Need Achievement in comparison to Gifted Underachievers.

The results of Table 09, and Fig. 2 & 3, analyzed and discussed factor-wise and on the composite score of Need Achievement in the above cited paragraphs, are in line with (Terman and Oden, 1947; Morgan, 1953; Gowan, 1957; Pierce, 1959; Pierce and Bown 1960; McClland, 1961; Mehdi, 1965; Hilderth, 1966; Zilli, 1971; Chaudhari, 1975; Havighurst, 1976; Whitemore, 1980; Francoys, 1985; Sternberg (1986), Devis and Rimm (1989); Chhaya, 1988; Maitra, 1991).

Terman and Oden (1947) have found that high Achievers had significantly more drive to achieve than low Achievers. Morgan (1952), while comparing a group of college Achievers and Underachievers of high ability, has revealed that the Achievers were self-confi ent and had more motivation to achieve than the non-Achievers. Gowan (1957), while summarizing some of the studies conducted on gifted Underachievers, concludes that lack of self-confidence is related to under achievement. Pierce (1959), on the characteristics of desire to achieve, has found that boys and girls of high achieving category valued achievement more than low achieving students. In a study conducted on high intelligent high/low Achievers Pierce and Bown (1960) have made it clear that high Achievers showed a higher achievement motivation than the low Achievers. High Achievers had greater expectation for academic success than the low Achievers. Those with strong achievement motivation generally do well in school and are self- reliant (McClland, 1961).

Hildreth, (1966), while identifying the major causes of underachievement, found that bright underachieving subjects gave top most priority to lack of effort to achieve. Zilli (1971) summarizing the literature attributed underachievement to five major causes of which inadequate motivation is the first one. Chaudhari (1975) has found that achievement motivation of bright Achievers was higher than the bright Underachievers. Havighrust (1976) has given a list of some characteristics for able Underachievers and the 2nd in priority is low aspiration level of Underachievers. Whitmore (1980), while summarising some of the characteristics of gifted Underachievers, enlists four characteristics as attributes of gifted Underachievers which are related to the need achievement - tendencies to continually set goals and standards too high; lack of self confidence; tendency to attribute success or failure to external control and lack of academic initiative. Several factors that can act as catalysts for actualization of giftedness in specific talents are said to be, particularly, motivation and environmental quality (Francoys, 1985). Sternberg (1986) has found that gifted Underachievers are characterized by lack of motivation, lack of perservance, too little or too much self-confidence and possess task completion problems. Chhaya (1988) has found that lack of self confidence is the characteristic feature of gifted Underachievers. Davis and Rimm (1989) has found that most important handicapping factor for gifted Underachievers is lack of achievement motivation. There is a significant relationship between academic underachievement and achievement motivation for gifted Underachievers (Maitra, 1991).

Keeping in view the results of all the studies mentioned above, it can be asserted with confidence that gifted Achievers differ from gifted Underachievers on Need Achievement. The results of the present study are in the expected direction. Therefore, the hypothesis No.

02 "In comparison to Gifted Underachiever, Gifted Achievers possess significantly high Need Achievement" is accepted.

Socio-economic Status:

For the measurement of socio-economic status Pareek and Trivedi's socio-economic status scale (Kashmiri adaptation by the present author), has been used and the results as shown in Table 10 and Fig. 4 are discussed as under:

It is evident from the perusal of Table 10 that Gifted Achievers have high socio-economic status while Gifted Underachievers possess low SES. The obtained 't' value 2.32 is greater than table 't' value at 0.05 level. Therefore, the results are statistically significant ($P<0.05$). The results confirm the supposition of the present investigator that low SES serves as a helping factor for underachievement. It also sounds right in the sense that when a child has no time to read and write at his home; has almost no academic facility in his family; shares the burden of the family in the form of helping his parents on fields; fights against poverty with his father in order to get two square meals for himself and other family members; utilizes his vacations on labour, so as to purchase books, notebooks and uniform; how can we expect his achievement to commensurate with his intellectual potential. Though in exceptional cases, it may not sound good, yet the decision is to be taken on average basis. It is more than obvious that the gifted with low SES have to become Underachievers in the school, because when their intellectual potential does not get proper environment, facility and above all time, it is certain that despite their high intellectual potential they will underachieve.

The results of the present study are further substantiated by Fig. 4. The perusal of the Figure makes it obvious for even a layman that two groups gifted

Achievers and Underachievers differ on SES. Gifted Achievers have decidedly a better SES in comparison to gifted Underachievers.

The results analysed and discussed in the above paragraphs are in line with Lidhoo and Khan (1990) who have found bright Underachievers have poor home backgrounds; Havighrust (1976) who, while summarising the characteristics of able Underachievers, has also attributed underachievement to low SES of the family. Menon (1972) who has made it clear that over and under achievement among high ability students is markedly influenced by SES. The results are in contradiction with Curry (1962) who has found that SES sems to have no effect on scholastic achievement of 6th grade students when the students have high intellectual ability. The results of authors except Curry (1962) justify that the results of the present study are in the expected direction. However, the study of Curry has been conducted on 6th class students when usually their tender hands can not help the father to supplement the family income. And as a matter of fact the child can devote his time towards his studies. But in the present study the sample subjects were 9th and 10th class students, who can help the father in order to boost the family income.

Keeping the above discussion in view hypothesis No-03 "The SES of Gifted Achievers is significantly better than Gifted Underachievers" is retained.

Factor analysis

Factor analysis is a method for determining the number and nature of the underlying variables among large number of measures. The purpose of factor analysis is not to predict the occurrence of phenomena, but to analyze the factorial composition of the mass of data. "Factor analysis serves the cause of scientific parsimony. It reduces the multiplicity of tests and measures to greater simplicity. It tells us in effect, what tests or measures belong together - which ones virtually measure the same thing in other words, and how much they do so. It thus reduces the number of variables with which the scientists must cope. It also helps the scientists locate and identify unities or fundamental properties underlying tests and measures". (Kerlinger, 1986 P.569). There are strong Unitary factorial structures underlying measures of Personality factors dimensions of Need Achievement and Socio-economic Status, separately for both Gifted Achievers and Underachievers. To test this intention the data regarding twenty one variables used in the study were subjected to factor analysis both for Gifted Achievers and Underachievers respectively. The list of the names of twentyone variables and their variable numbers are given in the Table 11.

Correlation Matrix - Gifted Achievers Group (N = 128)

A correlation matrix (21 x 21) has been presented in table 12 for the measures of twentyone variables. Considering the correlation matrix, it was found that it contains 210 correlation co-efficients. There were 90 negative co-efficients of correlation and remaining 120 positive. The magnitudes of co-efficients of correlation were found ranging from -0.3275 to 0.3148. Out of total 28 co-efficients of correlation, twelve co-efficients of correlation were significant at 0.01 level and 16 co-efficients of correlation were significant at 0.05 level.

Obtaining the factors - Gifted Achievers Group (N=128)

Through factor analysis performed on the inter correlation matrix (21x21), using principal component method (Hotelling, 1933) with varimax rotation (Kaisar, 1958), nine factors were extracted. The rotated factor matrix of the variables for the Gifted Achievers group along with communalities i.e. h2 has been presented in Tabled 13. These factors alongwith their Eigen values, percentage of total variance and cumulative percentage of total variance have been presented in table 14.

The table depicts that these factors collectively accounted for 64.5% of total variance. Factor - OIA with highest 11.3% and factor -09A 05% of the total variance.

Interpretation and Discussion of Factors - Gifted Achievers Group (N = 128).

Only loadings of 0.30 or above have been considered for interpretation and below this level ignored.

It is evident from the table 15 that factor-OIA runs through 05 variables (with significant loadings) and all are personality dimensions as measured by HSPQ. These are uncontrolled vs controlled, emotionally less stable vs emotionally stable, low super-ego strength vs high super-ego strength, dull vs bright, reserved vs warmhearted. Cumulatively these factors refer to the adjustment aspect of human personality. Therefore, this factor was named as "Adjustment". This factor accounts for 11.3% of the total variance with an eigen value of 2.381 as shown in Table 14.

Table 16 makes it obvious that factor - 02A has significant loadings on four variables: incomplete, reserved vs warmhearted, perseverance, internal control of fate. Two variables - incomplete and reserved vs warmhearted have positive loadings and two perseverance and internal control of fate negative loadings. This makes it bi-polar factor. There is a thread that goes on through almost all the four variables, that is, either satisfaction or dis-satisfaction. Therefore, it has been named as "Satisfaction vs Dissatisfaction". This factor accounts for 8.3% of the total variance with eigen value of 1.733 as depicted by table 14.

Table 17 shows the constellation of 05 variables: realistic attitude, hope of success, dull vs bright, untroubled state vs guilt proneness, internal control of fate on factor - O3A. Three variables have positive loadings - realistic attitude, hope of success, dull vs bright and two have negative - untroubled state vs guilt proneness, internal control of fate. All the variables almost are predominated by optimism. Therefore, the factor has been named as "Optimism". The factor accounts for 7.9% of the total variance with an eigen value of 1.767 as is obvious from table 14.

The perusal of the table 18 makes it clear that 05 variables have significant loading on factor - 04A, three variables: sound follower vs the person who prefers his own decision, dull vs bright and relaxed vs tense have positive loadings and two variables: tough minded vs tenderminded, reserved vs warmhearted, possess negative loading. These variables on one side depict self reliance and on the other side tension and apprehension. Therefore the factor was designated as "Self Reliant-cum-Apprehensive", the factor contributes for 7.4% of the total variance with an eigen value of 1.559 as shown in table 14.

From table 19 it is clear that three variables have high loadings on factor - 05A. Two variables have significant but positive loadings on variables: shy vs adventurous, relaxed vs tense and one variable: obedient vs aggressive negative loading. The variables demonstrate a trend of adventurousness and sensitivity simultaneously. Therefore, the factor was named accordingly "Advanturous-cum-Sensitive". The factor accounts for 07% of the total variance with an eign value of 1.463, as exhibited in table 14.

Table 20 depicts that high ego-Ideal, sound follower vs one who prefers his own decision have significant and positive loading, while likes group action vs internally restrained and realistic attitude have significant but negative loadings on factor - 06A. The factor has two positive and two negative loadings. Therefore, is designated as a bipolar factor. The common thread that runs almost through all the variables is high level of aspiration and group dependence simultaneously. Therefore, the factor is named as "High level of Aspiration-cum-Group Dependence". As shown in Tabled 14 this factor accounts for 6.3% of the total variance with an eigen value of 1.326.

Factor - 07A is represented by two variables with significant loadings: one serious vs happy-go-lucky with positive loading and the other high ego-ideal with negative. Therefore, it is a bipolar item. Constellation of first variable with the negative pole of high ego-ideal indicates calmness and this factor has been qualified as "Calm vs Enthusiastic". It accounts for 5.8% of the total variance with an eigen value of 1.215 as is evident from table 14.

The perusal of table 22 justifies that three variables have significant loadings on factor - 08A. Two factors have very high loadings: one socio-economic status and other internal control of fate and both have positive loadings. while the third variable - sound follower vs one who prefers his own decision, has moderate and negative loading. Taking the constellation of all the three variables into account, the factor has been named as "Social Status-cum-Self-determination". The factor accounts for 5.5% of the total variance and has an eigen value of 1.160 as is obvious from table 14.

Table 23 depicts that four variables constellate together with significant loadings on factor - 09A. Three variables, one undemonstrative vs excitable with very high loading and the other two sound follower vs one who prefers his own decision and internal control of fate with moderate but positive loadings. And one variable realistic attitude has negative but moderate loadings. A thread that goes through all the variables, connects them either through excitability or committedness. With the result the factor has been designated as "Excitable-cum-Committed". The factor accounts for 5% of the total variance and is the last factor that has an eigen value more than 01 i.e. 1.047. After this factor no extraction was possible as eigen value was less than 01 for the next factor.

Fig. 5 depicts the percentage of variance as shown in Table 14, regarding all the nine factors extracted in the gifted Achievers group. The percentage of variance has been converted into degrees and shown in the Fig. 5. All the nine factors account for 232.20^{o} (64.5%) out of total 360° (100%) of variance. Factor -01A "Adjustment" accounts for 40.68^{o} (11.3%), factor -02A "Satisfaction vs Dissatisfaction", 29.88^{o} (8.3%), factor - 03A "Optimism", 28.44^{o} (7.9%), factor - 04A "Self Reliant-cum-Apprehensive", 26.64^{o} (7.4%), factor - 05A "Advanturous-cum-Sensitive", 25.20^{o} (7.0%), factor - 06A "High level of Aspiration-cum-Group Dependent" 22.68^{o} (6.3%), Factor - 07A "Calm vs Enthusiastic", 20.88^{o} (5.8%), factor - 08A "Social Status-cum-Self Determination", 19.80^{o}(5.5%), factor - 09A "Excitable cum-Committed", 18° (5.0%) of variance.

Correlation Matrix-Gifted Underachievers Group (N=100)

A correlation matrix (21x21) was presented in Table 24 for measures of twenty-one variables. Considering the correlation matrix, it was found that it contained 210 correlation co-efficients. There were 120 positive co-efficients of correlation and the remaining 90 negative. The magnitude of co-efficients of correlation ranged from -.3274 to +.3148. Out of seventeen significant co-efficients of correlation 07 were significant at .01 level and 10 at .05 level.

Obtaining the Factors - Gifted and Underachievers Group (N=100)

Through Factor analysis performed on the inter-correlation matrix (21x21), using principal component method (Hotelling, 1933), with Varimax rotation (Kaiser, 1958), nine factors were extracted. The rotated factor matrix of the variables of the Gifted Underachievers group along with communalities (h2) has been presented in Table 25. The extracted factors along with their eigen values, percentage of total variance and cumulative percentage of total variance have been presented in table 26. The table depicts that these factors together accounted for 65% of the total variance. Factor -01U with highest 13.3% and Factor -09U lowest 4.9% of the total variance.

Interpretation and Discussion of Factors - Gifted Underachievers Group (N=100).

The loadings of 0.30 or above have been considered for interpretation and below this level have been ignored. The factors have been interpreted and discussed as under:-

The perusal of Table 27 makes it clear that on factor -01U there is a constellation of six variables with significant loadings. Three variables shy vs venturesome, uncontrolled vs controlled, low super-ego strength vs high super-ego strength have positive loadings and three variables - obedient vs aggressive, incomplete and likes group action vs internally restrained with negative loadings. Therefore, it is a bipolar factor. In almost three variables extroversion runs through and in the remaining three Introversion. Therefore, it has been named as "Extroversion vs Introversion" factor. It accounts for

13.3% of the total variance representing an eigen value of 2.787, as is obvious from table 26.

It is evident from table 28 that five variables have significant loadings on factor - 02U. All the factor loadings are positive, and aspiration and surgency runs through all the six variables - realistic attitude, Hope of Success, low super-ego strength vs high super-ego strength, serious vs happy-go-lucky and likes group action vs internally restrained. And as a matter of fact, the factor has been designated as "Aspirant-cum-Happy-go Lucky". The factor contributes for 8.3% of the total variance with an eigen value of 1.746 as is shown in Table 26.

Table 29 exhibits factor -03U representing five variables: internal control of fate, high ego-ideal, dull vs bright, uncontrolled vs controlled and likes group actions vs internally controlled with all significant and positive loadings. All the variables reflect pragmatic and individualistic trend in common. Therefore, the constellation of variables has been labeled as "Pragmatic-cum-Individualistic". The factor accounts for 7.7% of the total variance and has an eigen value of 1.608 as depicted in table 26.

The perusal of table 30 makes it obvious that factor -04U is represented by six variables with significant loadings. Four variables: undemonstrative vs excitable high ego-ideal, perseverance and low-ego strength vs high ego-strength, have reflected positive loadings and the other two variables: uncontrolled vs controlled and hope of success represent negative loadings. Undemonstrative vs excitable and high ego-ideal exhibit a high loading and thus serve as primary markers for factor -04U. All the six variables are characterized either by excitability or have an egoistic overtone. Therefore, the factor has been designated as "Excitable-cum-Egoistic". The factor accounts for 7.3% of the total variance and has an eigen value of 1.539, as is evident from table 26.

Factor -05U runs through four variables, three of them with positive significant loadings - emotionally less stable vs emotionally stable, shy vs adventurous, low super-ego strength vs high super-ego strength,and one, untroubled vs guilt proneness representing negative but significant loading as shown in table 31. On the one hand, the constellation of the variables represents calmness of personality and on the other hand adventurous side of the personality is referred to. Taking both the points into consideration, the factor has been labeled as "Placid-cum-Adventurous". the factor accounts for 6.6% of the total variance with an eigen value of 1.384, as depicted in table 26.

The table 32 makes it obvious that there is a constellation of three variables on factor - 06U two variables, tough minded vs tenderminded and relaxed vs tense have significant positive loadings and the one dull vs bright has significant negative loading. Tough minded vs tenderminded variable has a very high loading (0.87378) and therefore, serves as a primary marker for factor -06U. Dependence, over protectiveness, sensitivity, apprehensiveness and loneliness are the characteristic features of this factor and thus it has been named as "Sensitive-cum-Tense" factor. It contributes 6% of the total variance and represents an eigen value of 1.252, as is shown in table 26.

Table 33 indicates that factor - 07U runs through two variables with high significant loadings of 0.78085 and 0.69123 respectively. Both these variables, reserved vs warmhearted and serious vs happy-go-lucky, point out socio-interactional characteristics of personality like participating, easy going, attentive to people, trustful, cheerful, quick, alert, talkative and, therefore, the factor has been labeled as "Sociability". The factor explains

5.8% of the total variance and represents an eigen value of 1.219, as referred to in Table 26.

The table 34 makes it clear that factor - 08U is the constellation of three variables having significant loadings. The variables: sound follower vs one who prefers his own decision and perseverance represent positive loadings and the variable incomplete negative loading. Cumulatively all the three variables refer to a common thread i.e. own decision. Therefore, the factor was named as "Decisive". As shown in table 26 the factor accounts for 5.1% of the total variance with an eigen value of 1.077.

Factor - 09U is characterized by very high loading (0.86200) on variable socio-economic status and moderate loadings 0.36868, 0.34530, 0.30291 respectively on variables like emotionally less stable vs emotionally stable, relaxed vs tense, uncontrolled state vs guilt-proneness. The constellation of all the four variables on the factor has significant but positive loadings. Socio-economic status, bearing highest loadings, is the primary marker and the other three variables are dominated by emotionality. Therefore, the factor has been designated as "Social Status-cum-Emotional". The factor contributes 4.9% of the total variance and exhibits an eigen value of 1.034 as shown in Table 26.

The Figure 06 shows the percentage of variance, as depicted in Table 26, on all the nine factors extracted in the Gifted Underachievers group. The percentage of variance has been converted into degrees and shown in the Fig. 6. All the nine factors account for 234° (65%) out of 360° (100%) variance. Factor- 01U "Extroversion vs Introversion" accounts for 47.88° (13.3%), factor - 02U "Aspirant-cum-Happy-go-lucky", 29.88° (8.3%), factor - 03U "Pragmatic-cum-Individualistic" 27.72° (7.7%), factor - 04U "Exciable-cum-Egoistic" 26.28° (7.3%), factor

- 05U "Placid-cum-Adventurous" 23.76° (6.6%), factor 06U "Sensitive-cum-tense" 21.60° (6.0%), factor -07U "Sociability" 20.88° (5.8%), factor - 08U "Decisive" 18.36° (5.1%), factor - 09U "Social Status-cum-Emotional" 17.64° (4.9%) of variance.

A comparative view of the factor structure of Gifted Achievers and Underachievers shows that it is typical and specific to the two groups taken separately. The factor pattern in gifted Achievers is 01A Adjustment, 02A - Satisfaction vs Dissatisfaction, 03A - Optimism, 04A - Self reliat-cum-Apprehensive, 05A Advanturous-cum-Sensitive, 06A High level of Aspiration-cum-Group Dependent, 07A Calm vs Enthusiastic, 08A Social Status-cum-Self-determination, 09A - Excitable-cum-Committed. The inference can be drawn from the factor pattern that Gifted Achievers have better adjustment; Satisfaction and dissatisfaction runs through their behaviour; they are self-reliant but sometimes apprehensive; are adventurous but sensitive; have high level of aspiration but are simultaneously group dependent; are sometimes calm but preferably enthusiastic to do anything in life; are self-determined and maintain or better their social status, and are excitable but committed.

The factor pattern in Gifted Underachievers is 01U - Extroversion vs Introversion, 02U - Aspirant -cum-happy-go-lucky; 03U - Pragmatic-cum-Individualistic, 04U - Excitable-cum-Egoistic; 05U Placid cum-Adventurous; 06U-Sensitive-cum-Tense; 07U Sociability; 08U-Decisive; 09U - Social status-cum-Emotional. Inferences from the factor pattern can be drawn that Gifted Underachievers are characterised by extroversion vs Introversion simultaneously; are aspirant but deal with the task in hand in a happy-go-lucky manner; possess pragmatic qualities but at the same time are individualistic in their dealings; excitable to do the things in life but egoistic tendencies are dominant; calm and placid but adventurous in their style of life; sensitive but tense in their dealings; sociable, decisive in taking a decision right or wrong; inclined to improve or maintain their social status but at the same time emotional.

The factor pattern both for Gifted Achievers and Underachievers senses sound as one feels that different factor dimensions and constellations for two groups have emerged, differentiating them in a logical manner. Respective factor structures both for Gifted Achievers and Underachievers justify the discrimination between Gifted Achievement and Underachievement.

The results of the present study regarding factor analysis are in line with Maitra (1985); who has found in her study that gifted overAchievers were seen to be more conformist than gifted Underachievers, gifted Underachievers relied more on luck or fate as compared to gifted overAchievers and seemed to be less optimistic; Whitemore (1980) has characterised gifted under-Achievers who exhibit traits like poor execution of work, lack of concentration, setting unrealistic goals too high or too low; Prngle (1970) has found that the gifted Underachievers have more emotional problems; Purkey (1969), who has reviewed the literature on underachieving gifted, has given third priority to lack of perseverance among five distilled categories of problems contributing to underachievement; Hildreth (1966), while identifying five major causes of underachievement, has given topmost priority to lack of effort to achieve; Taylor (1964), while reviewing the literature from 1933 to 1963 has summarised seven traits that distinguish overAchievers from Underachievers. The second discriminating trait according to him, was related to self value. The overachiever accepted himself, felt optimistic and self confident, seemed to be persistent and enduring while the Underachievers tend to be self derogatory, possess the feeling of inadequacy and to withdraw in order to be self-sufficient. The related seventh distinction was goal-oriented, the overachiever was more realistic and thus more successful and the underachiever was unrealistic in setting goals and thus perpetuated a sense of failure. Bledshoe and Garrison (1962) who have observed the typical underachiever, especially if gifted, believe that such an underachiever has a concept of himself as inadequate, helpless and worthless and is, therefore, always on the defensive in order to maintain his integrity. On the other hand high Achievers were found to be self-confident and assertive in facing the new and difficult tasks, functioning in an active, flexible, abstract and independent manner. Durr and Collier (1960), while comparing gifted Achievers and Underachievers, have found that low achieving gifted group showed a definite trend towards a less favourable personality pattern. And gifted low Achievers, on California Test of Personality, were found to exhibit withdrawing tendencies, nervous symptoms and lack of self reliance, a sense of personal worth, a sense of personal freedom and a feeling of belonging. The mental health analysis revealed that low achieving gifted children were more likely to show a behavioural immaturity, emotional instability, feeling of inadequacy and certain nervous symptoms than gifted high achieving students. The high Achievers had greater feeling of individual worth greater ability to persist and cope with their own emotional disturbances. Morgan (1952) has found that college achievement of high ability students is related to self-confidence and motivation to achieve Terman and Oden (1947) have found that gifted Achievers had significantly more drive to achieve and were better adjusted.

The findings of the present study regarding factor analysis are partly in line with (Baum, et al., 1995; Mufson et al, 1989, Kulshrestha, 1981; Menon, 1972,

Savage, 1966). The findings of Baum, et al. (1995) confirm that four factors contribute to the under-achievement of the High academic achievement potential Underachievers. The four factors are emotional issues; social and behavioural issues; lack of appropriate curriculum; learning disabilities and poor self regulation. Emotional issues were the most frequent primary factor, curriculum issues and learning disabilities/poor self regulation tie for second, and social/behavoural concerns was the least frequent factor. Mufson et al (1989) have found that bright Underachievers are less confident and less emotionally and socially mature. Kulshrestha (1981) has revealed through her study that bright undrAchievers, in mathematics, were more warm hearted than normal Achievers. And bright normal Achievers, in English, were more conscientious than bright Underachievers. Menon (1972) has found that overachieving group of superior ability was less extrovert and less maladjusted than Underachievers.

In view of the findings of the present study supported by the research outlined above, the hypothesis No. 04 "the factor pattern associated with Gifted Achievers is decidedly different from Gifted Underachievers" stands confirmed.

Conclusions and Suggestions

What the individual achieves affects what the learner becomes.

Goodlad

Basic Assumptions

he present study was undertaken with the following basic assumptions:-

a) Academic underachievement is a complex phenomenon, the etiology of which needs the exploration of the relative variables.

b) The variables which affect the achievement of the gifted subjects negatively and result in their underachievement are both static and alterable.

c) The variables which effect the achievement of gifted subjects and positively result into the expected level of achievement are static, alterable and liable to be strengthened.

d) The concern towards giftedness means the concern for gifted Achievers and Underachievers so as to spell out the static and alterable variables representing both the groups.

On these basic assumptions, the present study undertook a thorough analysis leading to the following conclusions:

Conclusions

I. Gifted Achievers have high super-ego strength, are responsible, conscientious, persistent, moralistic, emotionally disciplined, motivated by a sense of duty and concerned about moral standards and rules, while Gifted Underachievers possess low super-ego strength, are frivolous, self-indulgent, fickle, undependable and disregard obligations to people.

II. Gifted Achievers are untroubled, self-assured, secure, serene, self-confident, insensitive to people's approval and disapproval and have no fears; and conversely Gifted Underachievers have guilt proneness tendencies, are insecure, worrying, troubled, anxious, sensitive to people's approval and disapproval and possess phobic symptoms.

III. Gifted Achievers have high need achievement, possess hope of success, are optimistic, identify themselves with a successful authority and prefer intrinsic rewards when successful; have high ego-ideal, are self-confident, competitive, maintain their self respect and have a sense of striving to achieve a high position or status; possess perseverance, prefer difficult and challenging tasks, have a sense of devotion to work, a long term involvement with their future career and dislike idleness; have realistic attitude, take intermediate risks and plan in advance, are in favour of Internal control of fate and possess strong determination, and are consistent in their behaviour. Gifted Underachievers have low need achievement and are somewhat pessimistic and prefer external rewards when successful; possess low ego-ideal, hardly bother to have a high position or status, are not competitive, feel less concerned towards maintenance of self-respect; are not perseverant, do not prefer difficult and challenging tasks, are not committed to work, have short term involvement with their future career; have unrealistic attitude, take either high or low risks in life and do not plan in advance for doing anything in life, possess a feeling of external control of fate, rely more on superior unknown forces than on self effort in shaping their destiny and have weak determination and possess inconsistent behaviour.

IV. Gifted Achievers have high socio-economic status in compararison to Gifted Underachievers.

V. Factor pattern associated with gifted Achievers are adjustment, satisfaction vs dis-satisfaction, optimism, self reliant-cum-apprehensive, adventurous-cum-sensitive, high level of aspiration-cum-group dependent, calm vs enthusiastic, social status-cum-self-determination, excitable-cum-committed. On the other hand, Gifted Underachievers are characterised by different factor pattern like extroversion vs introverson, aspirant-cum-happy-go-lucky, pragmatic-cum-individualistic, excitable-cum-egoistic, placid-cum-adventurous, sensitive-cum-tense, sociability, decisive, social status-cum-emotional.

Inferential Suggestions

The findings of the present study reveal that there are certain factors which can be manipulated so as to improve the academic achievement of the Gifted

Underachievers and strengthen the academic achievement of the Gifted Achievers.

1. Gifted Underachievers should be identified in the early years of their schooling, through intelligence tests and some other non-cognitive measures such the ones as referred to in this study.
2. Precautions should be taken beforehand by teachers, counsellors and parents, so that the personality dynamics of the gifted does not get disturbed.
3. Acceptance of the Gifted Underachievers should be ascertained both through teachers and parents.
4. Need achievement of Gifted Achievers should be strengthened and that of the Underachievers increased.
5. It should be ascertained that the Gifted Underachievers boldly accept their socio-economic status.
6. Individual counselling, making use of appropriate intervention techniques, should be used in order to strengthen the factors associated with gifted achievement and alter the factors related to gifted underachievement.
7. Inservice teacher preparation should be facilitated for understanding the educational needs of the gifted, their personal characteristics, methods of teaching the gifted and curriculum content recommended for them so that the gifted underachievement will hardly appear.
8. The co-ordination of pupils, teachers, principal, parents should be sought by the guidance and counselling worker in order to plan intervention

programmes for gifted Underachievers. This co-ordination can go a long way in helping this precious human resource - the gifted to come forward and man various departments as leaders so that the nation can achieve the strides and on the other hand the underachieving phenomena will go on decreasing.

9. In the absence of a guidance and counselling worker, the teacher should act as `go between' for the family and the school so as to bring about desired changes in the behaviour of Gifted Underachievers.

10. The parents need to be concerned towards the needs of their wards not only in terms of physical comfort but also in terms of intellectual needs. Subjects in the school and home need emotional support, stimulating atmosphere and encouragement.

Suggestions for further Research

I. The study should be replicated on a large sample, on different grades and age groups in order to generalise the results.

II. The number of variables should be increased to cover some other areas of gifted underachievement more so concerning school atmosphere - curriculum content, teachers attitude, teaching methods etc.

III. Intensive case studies of some Gifted Achievers and Underachievers should be undertaken in order to derive objective inferences.

IV. Intervention programmes - Individual counselling, group counselling, by making use of different counselling techniques - directive, non-directive, psycho-analytic and behavioural, should be used separately to examine the effect on the achievement of gifted Underachievers.

V. The intensity of gifted underachievement should be studied, after providing the appropriate guidance and counselling to the gifted, at an early age.

VI. The study may be done on a sample of students, in the form of longitudinal type, to trace out the course and strength of underachievement, with and without intervention programmes.

VII. Remedial coaching for Underachievers should be conducted and its effect on underachievement within a time frame should be observed.

VIII. Reinforcement in the form of rewards and better grades should be used as a remedial technique to deal with Gifted Underachievers.

IX. Narration of the stories of great persons, who were poor but achieved high position in the society, should be used as an intervention technique for dealing with Gifted Underachievers, so that they will feel unconcerned about their low SES and more determined towards success. Later on its effect on the academic achievement and need achievement of the experimental group should be studied after a lapse of appropriate time.

X. Comparison of the incidence of the gifted underachievement should be done on a sample where parents are and are not aware about the gifted potential of their children.

XI. Similar study, as the present one should be conducted on a sample of girls, so as to examine the gender difference.

XII. A comparative study should be conducted on a rural and urban sample in order to find out the differences.

XIII. A comparative study should be conducted on teacher expectations of Gifted Achievers and Underachievers.

XIV. A comparative study on a sample of Gifted Achievers and Underachievers should be conducted taking into consideration their self-concept and study habits.

XV. Discussion as a teaching technique should be used on a sample of Gifted Underachievers in order to examine its effect on an experimental group. The control group should be taught through the traditional teaching technique -- lecture method.

References

Agarwal, S. K, 1975. A psycho–social study of Academic Under achievement at secondary school level in the state of Rajasthan Ph.D. Edu; Raj. U cit. in Buch. M.B. (ed.) *Third Survey of Research in Education*, pp.657-58 NCERT.

Albert, R. S., 1978. Observations and suggestions regarding giftedness, familiar Influences and achievement of eminence. *The Gifted Child Quarterly*, 22, 2, pp. 201-211.

Allport, G. W., 1961. Pattern and Growth in Personality. New York (2nd edn.): Hold, Rainehart and Winston.

Ames, G. and Archer, J., 1988. Achievement Goals in the classroom: Students' Learning Strategies and Motivation Process, *J. of Edu. Psy.* Vol. 80, No. 3, pp. 260-267.

Anastasi, A., 1958. *Differential Psychology Individual and Group Differences in Behaviour* (3rd ed.). New York, Macmillan Co.

Anastasi, A., 1960. Validation of Biographical inventory as a predictor of college success. College Entrance Board Monogram No.1, College Entrance Examination Board, New York, cit. in *J. Educational Trends*, vol.13., No. 1, Jan. 1978, P.15.

Anolik, S. A., 1979. Personality, family, educational and criminological characteristics of bright delinquents. *Psychological Reports,* 44, pp. 727-734.

Atkinson, J. W., 1958. *Motives in Fantasy, Action and Society.* Princeton: D Van Nostrand Co, INC.

Bachtold, L. M., 1969. Personality differences among high ability Underachievers. *J. Edu. Research,* 63, pp.16-18.

Baker, J. A., 1995. Depression and Suicidal ideation Among Academically Gifted Adolescents. *Gifted Child Quarterly* Vol. 39, No. 4, pp. 218-223.

Ballering, L. B. and Koch. A., 1984. Family Relations when a child is gifted. *The Gifted Child Quarterly,* 28, 3, pp. 140-143.

Barbe, W. G. and Chambers, N.S., 1964. The adjustment of gifted children in special classes. *Gifted child Quarterly,* 8, pp. 32-35.

Barnett L. B. and Durden W. G., 1993. Education Pattern of Academically Talented Youth. *Gifted Child Quarterly,* Vol. 37, No. 4, pp. 161-168.

Barton et al., 1972. Personality, Motivation and I .Q measures as predicators of school Achievement and Grades. A non technical Synopsis. *Psychol –Abstract,* 48,4,7877.

Barton, K. Dielman, T. E. and Cattell, R. B., 1972. Personality, motivation and IQ measures as predicators of school achievement and Grades. A Non-technical Synopsis. *Psychol. Abstract* 48, 47877.

Baum, et al., 1995. Reversing Underachievement: Creative Productivity as a Systematic Intervention. *Gifted Child Quarterly,* Vol. 39, No. 4, PP. 224-235.

Baum, S. M. et al., 1996. Talent Beyond Words: Identification of Potential Talent in Dance and Music in Elementary Students. *Gifted Child Quarterly,* Vol. 40, 93-101.

Baymer, F. B. and Patterson, C. H., 1960. A comparison of three Methods of Assisting Under-achieving High school students. *Journal of Counselling Psychology.* Vol. 7, No. 2. pp. 83-92.

References

Best, J. W., 1983. *Research in Education.* New Delhi: Prentice Hall of India.

Bhatnagar, A., 1976. Effect of individual Counselling on the Achievement of Bright Underachievers. Reprinted from *Indian Educational Review.* Oct. pp.10-18.

Bhatt, C., 1966. A study of gifted children A. G. Teachers College, Ahmedabad (NCERT Financed) cit. in. Buch, M. B. (Ed.) *First Survey of Research in Education.*

Bledsoe, J. C. and Garrison, K. G., 1962. *The self concept of Elementary School Children in relation to their academic achievement, intelligence, interests and manifest anxiety* Athans: University of Georgia.

Binet, A. and Simon. Th., 1905. Methods nouvelles Pour le diagnostic du niveau Intellectual des anormaux. Annae Psychol., 11, 191-244. Cit. in Anastasi, A. *Differential Psychology.* America: Macmillan Co.

Borland, J. H. and Wright L., 1994. Identifying Young Potentially Gitted Economically Disadvantaged Students. Gifted Child Quarterly. 38, 164-171.

Bose, K., 1988. The Concept of Talent. Cit. in Raina, M. K. and Gulati. S. (eds.) *Identification and Development of Talent.* PP. 3-12 NCERT.

Bouchet, N. and Falk, R. F., 2001. The Relationship among Giftedness, gender and over-excitability. *Gifted Child Quarterly,* 45, pp. 260-267.

Brumbaugh, F. N. and Roseo, B., 1971. The most Highly Gifted Children. *Parents and Children.* Vol. IX. No. 1, PP. 17-22.

Buros, O. K. (Ed.), 1965. *The Sixty Mental Measurement Yearbook.* New Jersy. Highland Park: Gryphon Press.

Byers, J. A., Whitesell, S. S., et al., 2004. Gifted Students Perceptions of the Academic and Social/emotional Effects of Homogenous and Heterogeneous Grouping. *Gifted Child Quarterly,* Vol. 48, No. 1, pp. 7-20.

Callahan, C. M. and Caldwell, M. S., 1993. Establishment of a National Data Bank on Identification and evaluation

Instruments. *Journal for the Education of the Gifted*, 16, 201-219.

Cattell, J. Mck, 1890. Mental Tests and Measurement. *Mind*, 15, 373-380.

Cattell, R. B., 1957, A Universal Index for Psychological factors. *Psychologia,* 1, 7-85.

Cattell, R. B., 1963. The theory of Fluid and Crystalized Intelligence: a crucial experiment, *J. Edu. Psy.* 5. 1-22

Cattell, R. B. (ed.), 1970. *Handbook of Modern Personality Theory.* Chicago: Aldine.

Cattell, R. B. and Cattell, M. D. L., 1976. *Handbook for the Jr. Sr. High School Personality Questionnaire (HSPQ).* New Delhi: The Psycho-Centre.

Cattell, R. B. and Sealy, A. P., 1965. The general relations of changes in Personality and interest to changes in school performance: an exploratory study. *Coop. Res. Proj.* . no. 111. Urbana, III: Laboratory of Personality Assessment and Group Behaviour, Univer. III.

Cattell, R.B., et al., 1961. *Prediction and understanding of the Effect of childrens interest upon performance.* cit. in Cattell R.B. and Cattell M.D.L. Handbook for the High School personality questionnaire, – LiOIS, IPAT (1969).

Chadha, N. K. and Chandna, Sunanda, 1990. Creativity, intelligence and scholastic achievement: A residual study; *Indian educational Review*, Vol. 25(3), 81-85 cit. In *fifty Survey of Research in Education*, Vol. I, p. 724, NCERT, New Delhi

Chain, D. W., 2004. Social Coping and Psychological Distress Among Chinese Gifted Students in Hong Kong. *Gifted Child Quarterly*, Vol. 48, No. 1, pp. 30-41.

Chapin, F. S., 1928. A quantitative scale for rating the home and the social Environment of middle class families in an urban Environment. - *A First Approximation to the Measurement of socio-Economic Status.* 19, pp.99-111.

Chaudhari, U. S., 1988. The nature of Talent and Education cit. in Raina M. K. and Gulati Sushma (Eds.).

Identification and Development of Talent, pp. 8-57, New Delhi: NCERT.

Chaudhari, V.P, 1975. Factors contributing to academic Underachievement. Ph.D. edu: Nag .U: Cit in, *Third Survey of Research in Education.* Buch, M. B. (Ed) NCERT. 1978-83, p. 660.

Chaudhry, P., 1989. Student Activism - A Factor Analytical Study. *Indian Journal of Psy.* 64(14). pp. 1-16.

Chauncey, M. R., 1929. The Relationship of The Factor to Achievement and Intelligence Test scores. *J. of Ed. Research*, 20, pp .88-90.

Chauvin, J. C. and Karnes, F. A., 1983. A leadership Profile of Secondary Gifted Students. Psy. Reports, *Bi-monthly J.* 53, pp. 1259-62.

Chhaya, M.P., 1988. Finding Gifted Children cit. In., Raina, M.K. and Gulati Sushma (Eds), *Identification and Development of Talent* NCERT pp. 67-73.

Chhikare, M.S., 1985. *An Investigation into the Relationship of Reasoning Abilities with Achievement of concepts in life sciences*, Ph.D., Edu., JMI.

Cohlar, M. J., 1941. Scholastic status of Achievers and Non-Achievers of Superior Intelligence. *J. of Edu. Psy* , 32, p.605.

Colangelo, et al., 1993. A comparison of Gifted Underachievers and Gifted High Achievers. *Gifted Child Quarterly,* Vol. 37, No. 4, pp. 155-160.

Colangelo, N. and Dettmann, D. F., 1983. A Review of Research on Parents and Families of Gifted Children. *Exceptional Children,* Vol. 50, No. 1

Cox, C.C., 1926. The Early Mental Traits of three Hundred Geniuses. Cit. In Terman, L. M. (Ed.) *Genetic Studies of Genius.* Vol. 2, Standard, California: Stand. U. Press.

Cramer, R. H., 1991. The Education of Gifted Children in the United States A Delphi Study. *Gifted Child Quarterly.* Vol. 35, No. 2, pp. 84-91.

Curry, R.L., 1962. The Effect of Socio–economic Status on the scholastic achievement of Sixth grade children. *British J. Edu. Psy*; 32, 46-49.

D' Lima, C. D., 1979. Differential study of High and Low Achievement Syndromes of a Select Group of Creatively Gifted and Intellectually Gifted Children in the city of Bombay, Ph.D. Edu., Bom. U., cit in, Buch, M. B. (Ed.) *Third Survey of Research in Education*, p. 663. New Delhi, NCERT.

Dave, I., 1988. Guidance and Counselling of the Gifted and the Talented. Cit. In Raina, M. K. and Gulati, S. (Eds.) *Identification and Development of Talent. pp.* 230-236. NCERT.

Davids, A., 1966. Psychological Characteristics of high school male and female potential scientists in comparison with academic Underachievers. *Psychology in the schools*; 3, 79- 87.

Davis, G. A. and Rimm, S.B. , 1985. *Education of the Gifted and Talented*, New Jersey: Prentice Hall.

Davis, G. A. and Rimm, S. B., 1985. *Education of the Gifted and Talented*, New Jersey: Printice Hall.

Deb, Grewal, 1990. Relationship with regard to study habits and academic achievement of undergraduate home science final year students. *Indian Educational Review*, Vol.. 25(3): 7174.

Delise, J., et al., 1987. Preventing discipline problems with gifted students. *Teaching Exceptional Children*, 19, 4, 32-38.

Dennis, W. and Dennis, W. D., 1976. *The Intellectually Gifted: An Overview.* (Ed.) New Y: Grune and Stratton.

Deo, P., 1978. *Identification of Gifted Adolescents.* New Delhi: NCERT.

Desppande, A.S., 1984. A study of determinants of achievement of students at the SSC Examination in the Pune Division of Maharashtra State, Ph.D. Edu., Puna U.; cit in, Buch, M. B. (Ed.) *Fourth Survey of Research in Education.* Pp. 819-20, New Delhi: NCERT.

Deshpande, S., 1986. Interactive Effects of Intelligence and socio economic status of students and home work on the Achievement of students, Department of Education Kar. U; cit in, Buch M.B (Ed) *Fourth Survey of Research in Education,* 1983-88, Vol. I, p.820. NCERT.

Devi, Ujwala A., 1990. Pupil's academic achievement in relation to their intelligence, neuroticism and locus of control. M. Phil Edu. Annamalai Univ. cit in *Fifty Survey of Research in Education,* Vol. I, p. 724, NCERT, New Delhi.

Dhaliwal, A. S., 1971. *A study of some Factors contributing to Academic success and Failure among High school students – personality correlates of Academic over – Under–achievement.* Ph.D. Thesis, AMU library.

Dooley, L., 1916. Psychoanalytic Studies of Genius. *Ameri J. Psychol.*, 27, pp 363-417.

Drew, Elizebth, 1957. A four year study of Gifted Adolescents. Presented to the APA, DEC., 1957 Mimeo report, cit. In Gallaghar, J. J. *Analysis of Research on the Education of Gifted Children.* State of Illinois. Office of the Superintendent of Public Instruction (1960)

Durr, W. K. and Collier, C. C., 1960. Recent Research on the Gifted Education. 81, 163-169 cit. In., Whitemore, J. R. *Giftedness Conflict and Underachievement* Boston: Alleyn and Bacon Inc.

Ediger, M., 1987, Teaching the Gifted in The Science Curriculum. *The Progres of Edu. Sep. pp. 26-30.*

Entwistle, N. J. and Cunningham, S., 1968, Neuroticism and school Attachment :A Linear relationship. *Br. J. Ed. Psychol*; 38, pp. 123-132.

Entwistle, N. J. and Cunningham, S., 1970, The relationship between Personality, study Methods and Academic Performace *Br. J. Ed. Psychool.* 40, pp. 132-143.

Erikson, H., 1963, *Childhood and Society.* New York: Norton (2nd Ed.)

Eyench, H. J., 1953, *The Structure of Human Personality.* London: Methuen.

Eysench, H. J., 1952, *The Scientific Study of Personality*, London: Routledge and Kegan Paul

Feldman, D. H., 1984, A follow up of subjects scoring above 180 IQ in Terman's "Genetic Studies of Genius" *Exceptional Children*. Vol. 50. No. 6, pp. 518-555.

Feldman, D. H., 1993, Child Prodigies: A Distinctive Form of Giftedness. *Gifted Child Quarterly*, Vol. 37, No. 4, pp. 188-193.

Flemings, W.W.M., 1985, Attribution styles of Gifted High and Low Achieving Adolescents. *Dissertation Abstracts International*. Vol. 45, No. 07, P. 2048-A.

Francoys, G., 1985, Giftedness and Talent: Reexaming a Re-examination of the Definitions. *Gifted Child Quarterly*, Vol.. 29(3). Pp. 103-112.

Freehill, M. F., 1961, *Gifted Children: Their Psychology and Education*. N. York: Macmillan Pub. Co.

Freeman ,C. , 1961, Economic status and Adoption of new Agricultural and home practices cit .in Sexena, R. N. (Ed.) *Sociology, Social Research and social problems in India*: Bombay: Asia Publishing House.

Freeman, F. N. , 1942, *Mental Tests*, New York, Renold Press.

Freeman, J. , 1979, *Gifted children: Their Identification and Development in a social Context*, Baltimore: MTP press Lancester and University Park Press.

Freud, S., 1925, The relation of the poet to day-dreaming. Collected papers. Vol. IV. N.Y: Internet. Spychoanal. Press cit. In, Anastasi, A. *Differential Psychology*. The Macmillan Co. pp. 417-418.

Freud, S., 1933, *New Introductory Lectures on Psychanalysis*. New York. Norton.

Frierson, E. C., 1965, Upper and lower status gifted children: A study of differences. *Exceptional Children*. 32, pp. 83-90.

Fruchter, B., 1967, *Introduction to Factor Analysis*. New York: D. Van Nostrand Co. Inc.

References

Gallagher, J. J., 1960, *Analysis of Research on the Education of Gifted Children.* Springfield, 111: office of the Superintendent of public Instruction. pp. 42-43.

Gallagher, J. J., 1976, The gifted child in Elementary School. Cit. In., Dennis, W. and Dennis M. W. (Eds.) *The Intellectually Gifted: An Overview.* New York: Grune and Stration. Pp. 119-140.

Gallagher, J. J., 1988, National Agenda for Educating Gifted students: Statement of Priorities. *Exceptional Children.* Vol. 55, No. 2, pp. 107-114. Oct.

Gallagher, J. J., 1991, Educational Reform, Values and Gifted Students. *Gifted Child Quarterly,* Vol. 35, No. 1, pp. 12-19.

Gallagher, J. J. and Rogge, W., 1966, The Gifted. *British J. of Psy.* Pp. 37-55.

Gallagher. J. J. , 1985, Teaching the Gifted Child (3rd ed.), Borton: Allyn & Bacon.

Galton, F., 1869, *Heriditary Genius.* London: Macmillan Co.

Gardner, J. W., 1984, *Excellence, Can we be equal and Excellent Too?* (2nd Ed.,) Bombay: Vikas, Feffer and Simons Ltd.

Garg, Chitra, 1992, A study of family relations; socio-economic status, intelligence as correlates of academic performance; some field evidences. Indian Educational Review, Vol. 27(3). 107-110 cit. In, *Fifty Survey of Research in Education 1988-92,* Vol. I, P. 724, NCERT, New Delhi.

Garrett, H. E., 1981, *Statistics in Psychology and Education.* Bombay: Vakils, Feffer and Simons Ltd.

Garrison, K.C. , 1932, The Relative Influence of Intelligence and socio–cultural Status Upon the Information possessed by First Grade children, *J. Soc. Psy.* 3, pp.362-367.

Gelcer, E., 1991, Families of Gifted Underachieving Boys as portrayed by their Parents. *International J. of Special Edu.*, Vol. 6, No. 1, pp. 64-74.

Ghuman, M. S., 1976. A study of aptitudes, Personality traits and Achievement Motivation of Academic overAchievers and Underachievers. Ph.D. Psy. Rsu. cit. In, Buch, M.B. (Ed). *Third Survey of Research in Education.* 1978-83. Pp. 664-665 NCERT.

Girija, P. R. , 1980, A study of Intellectual and Non Intellectual Factors in academic achievement of Advantaged and Disadvantaged students from professional colleges., Ph.D. Psy. Kar U. cit in Buch, M. B. (Ed.) *Fourth Survey of Research in Education*, 1983-88. Vol I, P.823, NCERT.

Glenn, P. G., 1978, The Relationship of Self-concept and IQ to Gifted students, expressed need for structure. *Dissertation Abst. International.* 38, 4091-A.

Gnanambal, T. S., 1987, Identification of Gifted Children. *Experiments in Edu..* Vol. XV, No. 11, pp. 223-227.

Goldman, L. (ed.), 1978), *Research Methods for Counsellors.* New York: John Willey and Sons.

Gosh, S. N., 1972, Non-Cognative Characteristics of Over and Under Achievers. A Review of Studies. *Indian Educational Review*, Vol. 7, No. 2, pp. 78-91.

Gowan, J. C., 1955, The underachieving Gifted Child: A Problem for every one. *Exceptional Children*, 21, 247-249.

Gowan, J.C. , 1957, Dynamics of the underachievement of Gifted Students. *Exceptional Children*, 24 Nov pp.98-101.

Gowan, J, C., 1960, Factors of Achievement in High school and college. *J. Counselling Psy.* 73, pp.91-95.

Green, K. et al., 1988, Family characteristics and under achieving Gifted Adolescent Males, *Gifted Child Quarterly*, Vol. 32, No.2, Spring.

Grossberg, I.N. & Cornell, D.G. , 1988, Relationship between Personality adjustment and high intelligence. Terman versus Holling worth. *Exceptional Children*, 55, No. 3, pp. 266-272.

Guildford, J. P., 1954, *Psychometric Methods.* Bombay: Tata McGraw Hill Publishing Co. Ltd.

References

Guildford, J. P., 1959, Three Faces of Intellect, *American Psychologist*, 14, pp. 469-479.

Guildford, J. P., 1965, *Fundamental Statistics in Psychology and Education.* New York: McGraw Hill.

Guilford, J. P., 1967, *The nature of human Intelligence.* New York: McGraw Hill.

Gupta, J. P., 1989, Education of the Gifted. *The Primary Teacher*, Vol. XIV. No. 3, pp. 18-21.

Haggard, E ., 1957, Socialisation, Personality and Academic Achievement in Gifted Children. *School Review.* 65: 388-414. Dec.

Hall C. S. and Lindzey G., 1989, *Theories of Personality.* New Delhi: Wiley Eastern Limited (3rd Edn.)

Hamilton, N. K., 1960, Special Educational Programmes for Gifted Children. *Exceptional Children*, 27, pp. 147-150.

Haq, Najmul, 1988, A study of Certain Personality Correlates of Over under-achievement in different subjects (Hindi, English, Math and Science) among male and female to investigate the sex differences of overAchievers and Underachievers in individual subject areaa along different personality dimensions. Ph.D., Education, AMU.

Harman, H. H., 1976, *Modern Factor Analysis.* (3rd Ed.), London: The University of Chicago Press.

Havighurst, R. J., 1976, Conditions Productive of superior children. cit. In; Dennis, W. and Dennis, M.W (Eds) *The Intellectually Gifted*, New York: Grune and Stratton.PP.251-261.

Herzberg, A., 1929, *Psychology of Philosophers.* N. Y. Harcourt, Brace.

Hickson, J., 1991, Understanding the Affective Needs of the Gifted. *International J. of Special Edu.*, Vol. 6, No. 1, pp. 34-44.

Hildreth, G. , 1966, *Introduction to the Gifted.* New York: McGraw Hill.

Hirsch, N. D.M., 1931, *Genuis and Creative Intelligence*, Cambridge, Mass: Sci. Art.

Hitschmann, E., 1956, *Greatmen: Psychoanalytic Studies.* N.Y. Intern Universities Press.

Holligworth, L. S., 1926, *Gifted Children: Their nature and nurture.* N. Y. Macmillein.

Hopkins, C. D., 1976, *Educational Research: A Structure for Inquiry.* Columbus, Ohio: Charles E. Merrill Publishing Company.

Horn, J. L., 1994, Theory of Fluid and Crystallized Intelligence. In R. J. Sternberg (Ed.). *The Encyclopedia of Human Intelligence* (Vol. 1, pp. 443-451), New York, Macmillan.

Hotelling, H., 1933, Analysis of a Complex of Statistical Variabies into Principal Components. *J. Educ. Psychol.*, 24, pp. 417-441 and pp. 498-520.

Hunsaker S. and Callahan, C., 1993, Evaluation of Gifted Programs: Current Practices. *Journal for the Education of the Gifted*, 16, 190-200.

Hurlock, E. B., 1976, *Personality Development.* New Delhi: Tata McGraw Hill.

Hussain, M. G., 1987, Giftedness and Motivation - a Study of Disadvantaged Minority. *Man and Development.* 9(2), pp. 1-11.

Iyer, K. K., 1977, Some Factors related to underachievement in Mathematics of Secondary School Students. Ph.D. Edu. Ker. U. cit in., Buch, M. B. (Ed.) *Third Survey of Research in Education*, 1978-83. P. 668, NCERT.

Jagannadhan, K., 1985, The effects of certain Socio-psychological factors on the Academic Achievement of Children studying in Classes V to VII, Ph.D. Edu., SVU, cit. In Buch, M. B. (Ed.). *Fourth Survey of Research in Education.* 1983-88, Vol. 1, p. 826, NCERT.

Jerome, K., 1984, Underachievement - The two type hypothesis. *Dissertation Abst., Internal, Human and Social Science, No. 3, P. 358.*

John, C. W., 1930, Educational Achievement in Relation to Intelligence. Cambridge: Harward University Press. Cit. In, Rao, S. N. (1970). A Study of some Factors related to

Scholastic Achievement. *Indian J. of Psy. 45(2), pp. 99-120.*

Joseph, T.T. , 1979, A study of some Predictors of Achievement in chemistry at the Pre-degree level. Ph.D. Edu; Ker. U; cit in Buch, M.B. (Ed). *Third Survey of Research in Education.* pp. 669-70. New Delhi: NCERT.

Jyothi,P., 1984, A study of Achievement Motivation in relation in Personality dimensions and performance among High and Low Achieving College Girls, *J. of Psycho. Research,* Vol. 28, No. 3, pp. 135--138.

Kaiser, H. F., 1958, The Varimax criterion for Analytic Rotation in Factor Analysis. *Psychometrika,* 23, pp. 187-200.

Kandu, R., 1988, Identification of Talent at School. Some constraints and remedies. Raina, M. K. and Gulati, S. (Ed.) *Identification and Development of Talent,* pp. 58-66. NCERT.

Kapoor, Rita , 1987, Study of factors Responsible for high and low Achievement at the junior High school level Ph.D Edu. Avadh cit in Buch M B (Ed). *Fourth Survey of Research in Education,* (1983-88), Vol. 1, pp.829–830 New Delhi, NCERT.

Kerlinger F.N., 1986, *Foundations of Behavioral Research.* New York: Holt Rinehart and Winston.

Kernes, M. B. Shwedel, A. M. and Levis, G. F., 1983, Short-term Effects of Early Programming for the Young Gifted Handicapped Child. *Exceptional Children,* Vol. 50, No. 2, pp. 103-109.

Kerr, B., Colangelo, N. and Gaeth, J., 1988, Gifted Adolescent's Attitudes Towards Their Giftedness. *Gifted Child Quarterly.* Vol. 32, No. 2, pp. 245-253.

Khan, M. A., 1986, A study of Parental Attitude and Personality Types of Gifted Children. *M.Phil. Dissertation* (Unpublished), University of Kashmir Library.

Khan, Mahmoda, A. , 1987, *The Effect of Individual counselling on the Achievement of Bright Underachievers* Unpublished M.Phil. dissertation, University of Kashmir Library.

Khan, Mahmood A. , 1995a, Gifted Achievers and Underachievers their Personality profiles, Need Achievement and Socio-Economic Status. *Indian Educational Review*, Vol. 31, No 2.

Khan, Mahmood, A., 1995. Kashmiri Adaptation of Pareek and Trivedi's Socio-economic Stauts Scale. *Insight*, Vol. 2, No. 2, pp. 28-36.

Khanna, M.A. , 1980, A study of the Relationship between students socio–economic back ground and their Academic achievement at Junior school level Ph.D Edu. Kan U. cit. in. Buch, M. B. (Ed.) *Third Survey of Research in Education*, p.671, NCERT.

King, J. E., 1948, Using tests in the modern secondary school. Bull. Nat. Assoc. Secondary School Principals 32: 158, 3-92. Cit. In Catell, R. B. and Cattell, M. D. *Handbook Jr. Sr. HSPQ* (1976) Psychocentre, New Delhi.

Kirk, S. A., 1962, *Educating Exceptional Children Boston: Houghton Mifflin. Co.*

Kohli, T. K., 1975, Characteristic Behavioural and Environmental correlates of Academic Achievement of Over and Underachievers at different levels of Intelligence, cit. In *J. Indian Education Review*. Vol. XX, No.1, Jan. 1985 P.110.

Kothari C.R., 1990, *Research Methodology Methods and Techniques* (2nd Ed.), New Delhi Wilay Eastern Limited.

Kotwadkar, V., 1980, Study of gifted children in relation to their personality variables, level of adjustment and scholastic achievement. Ph.D. Home science, Nagpur University, *5th Survey of Research in Education*, 1988-92, Vol. II, pp. 1882.

Koul, L., 1978, Personality Needs of High and low Achievers in Mathematics H.PU .Cit. In Buch, M. B,(Ed). *Third Survey of Research in Education*, 1978 –83 p. 671, New Delhi, NCERT.

Kretschmer, E., 1931, *The Psychology of men of Genius*. N. Y. Harcourt, Brace.

References

Kulshretha, L., 1981, A study of certain factors related to differential patterns of achievement among Bright Students. Ph. D . Edu., Aug., U; cit. in *Third Survey of Research in Education,* Buch, M.B. (Ed) NCERT 1978-83, pp. 671-672.

Kumar, Awadhesh, , 1986, A study of Ego-involvement, level of Aspiration and Associated factors in Relation to Achievement at Graduation level, Ph.D. Edu., Gor. U., cit. In Buch, M. B. (Ed.) *Fourth Survey of Research in Education 1983-88.* Vol. 1, p. 831, NCERT.

Kumar, G., 1988, Characteristics of the Gifted and talented. Raina, M. K. and Gulati, S. (Ed.) *Identification and Development of Talent,* pp. 95-107. NCERT.

Kuppuswamy, B., 1959, A scale to measure socio-economic status. *Ind. J. Psychol.* 34, pp. 1-10.

Lajoie, S. and Shore, B., 1981, Three myths? The over-representation of the gifted among dropouts, delinquents and suicides. *Gifted Child Quarterly,* 25, pp. 138-143.

Lange, Echbaum, W., 1932, *The Problem of Genius.* M.Y.: Macmillan.

Lange-Eichbaum, W., 1928, Ganie, Irrsinn und Ruhm. Munich: Rainhardt. Cit. In, Anastasi, A. *Differential Psychology.* N. Y: Macmillan Co, (1958)

Lange-Eochbaum, W., 1951, Das Genie - Problem: eine Einfuhrung. Munich: Reinhardt. Cit. In. Anastasi, A. *Differential Psychology.* N.T: Macmillan Co. (1958).

Lawrence, G. H., 1985, A study of the Differences in observable characteristics of learned Helplessness Demonstrated on a Reading Task by underachieving and Achieving Fourth, Fifty and Sixth Grade boys of low and high socio-economic status. *Dissertation Abstract International.* Vol. 45, No. 11, May.

Lehman, E. B. and Erdwins, C. J., 1981, The Socio and Emotional Adjustment of Young intellectual gifted children. *Gifted Child Quarterly,* 25, pp. 134-137.

Lewis, D and Dhillon. H. S. , 1955, *Leadership and Groups in a south India village.* Delhi: P.E.O Publication No.9, pp.146-148.

Lidhoo, M. L and Khan, Mahmood. A., 1990, Bright Underachievers among the socially Backward: Counselling and Remedial Measures, *India Educational Review,* Vol. XXV, No .1, Jan.

Lombroso, C., 1895, *The man of Genius.* N. Y: Scribner's.

Long, L. and Mehta, P. H. (Eds.), 1960, *First Mental Measurement Handbok of India.* New Delhi. NCERT Publication Centre.

Lyon, H., 1976, Realizing our potential cit. In Gibson, J. and Channels, P. (Eds.) *Gifted Children: Looking to their Future.* London: Latimer New Dimensions Ltd.

Madhosh, A. G. and Rafiqui, K. P. , 1990, *Manual of the socio-economic status scale (Rural and Urban),* Srinagar: Crown Press, Batamaloo.

Mahmahopaday and Byti, 1986, The concept of the gifted child; *The Educational Review,* XCII No 2, pp.15-16.

Maitra, K , 1993, *Gifted and Talented A Developmental Perspective.* New Delhi: Discovery Pub House.

Maitra, K , 1996, *Parenting the Gifted.* New Delhi Discovery Publishing House.

Maitra, K., 1985, Affective correlates of the gifted Underachievers. Ph.D. thesis Del. Uni. cit. in Buch, M.B.(Ed) *Fourth Survey of Research in Education,* 1983–88, New Delhi, NCERT Vol. I pp.834-835.

Maker, C. J., 1995, Identification of Gifted Minority Students: A National Problem, Needed Changes and a Promising Solution. *Gifted Child Quarterly,* 40, 41-50.

Malik, J. S., 1991, *Personality Factors and Learning Environments.* Udaipur: Himanshu Publications.

Marland, S. P., 1972, *Education of the gifted and the talented.* Report to the Congress of the United States by the U.S. Commissioner of Education and background papers submitted to the U.S. Office of Education. Washington, D.C.:U.S.

Mathur, Madhu, 1992, A study of spontaneous art of high and low Achievers. The study aims at exploring the differential characteristics in spontaneous art of high and low Achievers. *Ph.D.,* Education, Banasthali Vidapith. *5th Survey of Research in Education*, VII, pp. 1886.

Maitra, K. , 1991, *Gifted Underachievers a challenge in Education.* New Delhi; Discovery Publication House.

Mc Clelland ,R., 1989, Profile of underachieving gifted students Unpublished doctoral Dissertation University of Alberta, Edmonton cit in Wilgosh L. Underachievement and Related issues for culturally different Gifted children. *International J. of Special Education*, P.83.

McClelland, C.D., Atkinson, J. W., Clark, R. A. and Lowell, E. L., 1953. *The Achievement Motive,* New York: Appleton Century Crafts

McClland, C.D., 1961, *The Achieving Society.* Princeton, Van Nostrand.

McCoach, D. B. and Siegle Del, 2003, Factors that Differentiate Underachieving Gifted Students from High-Achieving Gifted Students, *Gifted Child Quarterly,* Vol 47, No. 2, pp. 144-154.

Mehdi, B., 1965, What Research has to say about underachieving among the Gifted. *Guidance Rev.,* 3,2.

Mehdi, B., 1987, Education for Talent Development - The Indian Scene. *J. of Indian Edu.*, Vol. 13, No. 3, Sept. pp. 8-14.

Mehna, V. H., 1986, An investigation into some factors Affecting Academic Achievement in Science of IX Standard students of Greater Bombay, Ph.D. Edu., Bom. U., cit. In Buch, M. B. (Ed.) *Fourth Survey of Research in Education.* 1983-88, Vol. I.

Mehrota ,S., 1986, A study of the Relationship between Intelligence socio-economic status, Anxiety, personality Adjustment and Academic Achievement of High school students Ph.D, Edu; Kan ,U. cit in, Buch, M. B. (Ed)

Fourth Survey of Research in Education, 1983-88. Vol. I, p. 836, NCERT.

Mehta, Prayag, 1967, Level of need achievement in high school boys. *Indian Edu., Review,* II 2, Nov.

Mehta, Prayag, 1969, The achievement Motive in High School Boys. *Research Monograph*, New Delhi: NCERT.

Menon, S. K ., 1972, A comparative study of personality characteristics of overAchievers and Underachievers of high ability. Ph.D. Psy: Ker.U: cit in Buch, M. B. (Ed.) *Third Survey of Research in Education.* NCERT 1978-83 P.674.

Miles, C.C., 1954, Gifted children. Cit. In L. Carmichael (Ed.) *Manual of Child Psychology* (2nd Ed.): New Wiley.

Mills, C. J. and Tissot, S. L., 1995, Identifying Academic Potential in Students from Under-represented Populations: Is Using the Ravens Progressive Matrices a good Idea? Gifted Child Quarterly, Vol. 39, No. 4, pp. 209-217.

Ministry of Education, 1964-1966, Report of the Education Commission. *Education and National Development.* Govt. of India, New Delhi, pp.240-241.

Ministry of Human Resource Development, 1986. *National Policy on Education. 1986,* Programme of Action, Ministry of Human Resources Development, Department of Education, New Delhi, pp.23-26.

Misra , M. , 1986, A critical study of the Influence of socio-economic status on Academic Achievement of Higher secondary students in Rural and urban Areas of Kanpur. Ph.D Edu Kan.U: cit in Buch, M.B. (Ed.) *Fourth Survey of Research in Education* 1983-88, Vol .I, p. 837, NCERT.

Miyan ,M., 1988, Foster Talent for a Better Future. Cit in, Raina M. K. and Gulati, S. Eds. *Identification and Development of Talent*, pp.132-140.

Mohan and Virdi, 1985, A study of Personality and Persistence. *Indian Psychological Review.* Vol. 28, No. 6, pp. 17-19.

Mohan, V and Khera, N. , 1978, The Relation of over and under –achievement to socio economic status and 16 P.F. in school children. *Educational Trends.* Vol. 13, No.1 pp..13-23.

Mohan, V. and Nehru, K., 1972. Differentiation of over and under-Achievers on 16 PF. *Psycho-Studies*, 17, pp. 52-53.

Moon, S. M., 1995, The Effects of an Enrichment Program on the Families of Participants: A Multiple Case Study. Gifted Child Quarterly, Vol. 39, No. 4, pp. 198-208.

Moon, S. M., 1996, Using the Purdue Three-stage Model to Facilitate Local Program Evaluations; *Gifted Child Quarterly,* No. 40, No. 3, pp. 121-128.

Moore, W. D., Hahn, W. G. and Brentnall, L. C., 1978, Academic Achievement of Gifted Children: A Comparative Approach. *Exceptional Children.* Vol. 44, No. 8, pp. 618-19. May.

Morgan, H. H., 1952, A psychometric comparison of Achieving and Non-achieving College students of High Ability. *J. Consult.Psy.* 16, 292-98.

Morrow, W.R. and Wilson, F.C., 1967, Family relations of bright high achieving and underachieving school boys. *Child Development*, 32., pp.507-510.

Mufson, L., et al., 1989, Factors Associated with under-achievement in Seventh Grade Children. *J. of Educational Research.* Vol. 83, Sept- Oct., No .01. pp. 5-10.

Mujerjee, B. N., 1977, *A letter sent by Mujerjee to Dr. Zargar, A. H.* on 25th of August, 1977. For the clarification of certain concepts.

Mukherjee, B. N., 1968, *Research Manual for Mukherjees Incomplete Sentence Blank,* Canada: York University, Toranto.

Mukherjee, S. and Mookherjee, D., 1969, Educational Provisions for the Gifted: A Review. *Indian Edu. Review.* Vol. 4, No. 1. 101-115.

Murray, H. A., 1938, *Explorations in Personality.* Oxford: The University Press.

Nagpal, R., 1979, A study of Non- Intellectual characteristics of over and underachieving Engineering students cit in, Buch M.B. (Ed). *Third Survey of Research in Education* Ph.D Human PP,677-78 New Delhi : NCERT.

Natesan, H. and Devi, K. R., 1987, A comparative study of the Personality Factors of High and Low Achievers. *J. of Edu. Research and Extension.* Vol. 24, No. 2, pp. 74-80.

Naylor, F. D., 1972, *Personality and Educational Achievement,* New York: John Wiley and Sons.

Oakland, I. A.., 1969, Measurement of Personality correlates of Academic Achievement in High school Students. *J. Counselling Psy.* 16, PP. 452-457.

Olszawski, P. et al. , 1987, The influence of the family environment on the development of talent: A Literature Review J, for the Edu .of the gifted. *J. for the Edu. Of the Gifted,* Vol. II (I), pp .6-28.

Oram, et al., 1995, Program Students. *Gifted Child Quarterly,* Vol. 39, No. 4, pp. 236-244.

Pacholi, S.P., 1980. Incidence of Under achievement at the Higher Secondary level. *Indian Edu, Review.* Vol. 14, No.2, pp.114 –119.

Pandey U.D and Singh, N. P., 1970. A correlation study of reading speed, Academic Achievement and Intelligence of university students, *J. Ed. and Psychol,* 28,3.

Pandey, A., 1980, A comparative study in the areas of adjustment between intellectually Bright and Average Higher Secondary adolescents. *Indian Edu. Research,* Vol. 14, No. 2, pp. 120-124.

Pareek U. and Trivedi, G, 1964, *Manual of the Socio-economic status scale (rural),* New Delhi : Manasayan.

Parker, J. P., 1996, In the public Interest NAGC Standards for Personnel Preparation in Gifted Education: A Brief History. *Gifted Child Quarterly,* Vol. 40, No. 3, pp. 158-161.

Parthasarathy, R., 1988, Identification and Development of Talent. Cit. In Raina, M. K. and Gulati, S. (Eds.)

Identification and Development of Talent. Pp. 274-281, NCERT.

Passi, B. K., 1997, A Trend Report on Creativity and Innovation. 170-215. Cit. In *Fifth Survey of Research in Education.* 1988-92, Vol. I.

Patel, A.S. and Joshi R. J., 1977, A study of adjustment process of high and low Achievers *J. of Psychological Researchers.* Vol. 21, No3.

Patel, M. M., Parikh, J. C. and Patel, S. T., 1984, A study of Identification Patterns and Academic Achievement of Talented studnets. *Indian J. of Psychology.* Vol. 59, No. 1 and 2, pp. 40-48.

Pathak, C.C., 1974, A study of Achievement Motive, Educational Norms and School Performance of High School Pupils, Ph.D. thesis SPU. Cit. In Buch, M. B. (Ed.) *Second Survey of Research in Education,* Baroda SERD, PP. 190-191.

Pendarris, E. D., et al., 1990, *The Abilities of Gifted Children.* Prentice Hall New Jersy, Englewood Cliffs.

Pervin, L A., 1970, *Personality: Theory and Research.* New York: John Wiley and Sons.

Peterson, D., 1977, The heterogenously gifted child. *Gifted Child Quaterly.* 21, pp. 396-408.

Piaget, J. and Inhelder, B., 1969, *The Psychology of the Child.* New York: Basic Books.

Pierce, J. V., 1962, The Bright Achiever and underachiever: A Comparison. *The Gifted Child. The Yearbook of Education.* (Ed.) Bereday, G.Z.F. Lawerys, J. A. new York: Harcourt Brace and World, INC. pp. 143-154.

Pierce, J. V. and Bowman, P.U., 1960, Motivation pattern of superior high school students and the gifted students. Cooperative Research, U.s. Department of Health, education and Welfare, Office of the Education, Washington, D.C. cit. In, Maitra, Krishna: *Gifted Underachievers - A Challenge in education.* Discovery Publishing House. New Delhi. Pp. 75-76.

Pirece, J. V., 1959, The Educational Motivation Patterns of Superior Students who do and do not Achieve in high school. Mimeo report, University of Chichgo, cit. In *Analysis of Research on the Education of the Gifted Children*. Jallagher, J. J. State of Illinois: Office of the Superintendent of Public Instructions (1960). Pp. 35-36.

Pringle, M. L., 1970, *Able misfits*. London: Longman Group.

Purcell, J. H., 1993., The Effects of the Elimination of Gifted and Talented Programs on Participating Students and their Parents. *Gifted Child Quarterly*, Vol. 37, No. 4, pp. 177-187.

Puri, K., 1987, Personality Traits and self concept of 16-18 year old Underachievers. Ph.D Edu. cit in Buch, M.B (Ed.) *Fourth Survey of Research in Education* (1983-88). Vol 1, New Delhi. NCERT, p.845.

Purkey, W.W., 1969. Project self discovery, its effects on bright but underachieving high school students. *Gifted Child Quarterly*, 123,242-246.

Pyryt M. C. and Mendaglio, S., 1994. The Multi-dimensional Self Concept: A Comparison of Gifted and Average-ability Adolescents. *Journal for the Education of the Gifted*, 17, 299-305.

Radhakrishnan, S., 1949. *Report of the University Education Commission*, 1948-49. Delhi, Manager of Publications.

Rai, P. N., 1980. Achievement Motives in Low and High Achievers: A Comparative Study. *Indian Education Review*: Vol. 14, No. 3, pp. 117-123.

Rai, P. N., 1982. A comparative Study of a few Differential Personality Correlates of low and high Achievers, *Indian Dissertation Abstracts*. July-Dec.

Raina, M. K., 1988. Perspectives and Future Possibilities in the Education of the Gifted and the Talented, cit. In Raina, M. K. and Gulati, S. (Ed.) *Identification and Development of Talent*. Pp. 312-328. NCERT.

Raina, M. K., 1988a. Concept and Identification of Talent. Cit., in Raina, M. K. and Gulati, S. (Eds.) *Identification and Development of Talent*, New Delhi: NCERT.

Raina, M.K and Gulati, S., 1988. *Identification and Development of Talent*, New Delhi: NCERT.

Rajput, A. S., 1984. Study of Academic Achievement of students in Mathematics in Relation to their Intelligence Achievement ,Motivation and socio-economic status Ph.D. Edu; Pan U; in Buch M.B.(Ed) *Fourth Survey of Research in Education.* 1983-88, Vol. I p. 845, NCERT.

Rajyaguru, Mahesh S., 1991. A comparative study of over and under-Achievers in Maths to compare the achievement in Maths, personal characteristics and environmental characteristics, overAchievers and Underachievers in Maths. Ph.D. Education, Bhavnagar University, *5th Survey of Research in Education*, VII, pp. 1902.

Ralph, et al., 1966. *Bright Underachievers*. New York: Teachers College.

Rao, S. N., 1963. *Students Performance and Adjustment.* A Pub. Ph.D. thesis, Tirupati: S. V. University (S. India), p. 10.

Ravens, J. C., 1962. Advanced Progressive Matrices, Set I and II Instructions, Scoring Key and Norms; London: H.K. Lewis and Co.

Reis, S. M. and Renzulli, J. S., 1991. The Reform Movement and the Quiet Crisis in Gifted Education. *Gifted Edu. Quarterly.* Vol. 35, No. 1, PP. 26-35.

Renzulli, J. S., 1988. The Multiple Menu Model for Developing Differentiated Curriculum, for the Gifted and Talented. *Gifted Child Quarterly,* Vol. 32, No. 3, pp. 298-309.

Rimm, S.B. and Lowe, B., 1988. Family environments of underachieving gifted children. *Gifted Child Quarterly,* 32,No. 4, Fall 11, 353-359.

Roe, Anne, 1952. A Psaychologist Examines 64 Eminent scientists. *Scientific America.* 187: pp. 21-25.

Roe, Anne, 1952a. *The Making of a Scientist*, New York: Dodd, Mead.

Rossman, J., 1931. *The Psychology of the Inventor.* Washington D.C.: Inventors Publ. Co.

Rost, D. H. and Czeschlik, T., 1994. The Psycho-social Adjustment of Gifted Children in Middle Childhood. *European Journal of Psychology of Education*, 9(1), 15-25.

Sahoo, R., 1987. Reading Achievement and verbal Processing Ability of Achieving and Non-achieving Readers, Ph.D. Psy. Cit In: Buch M.B. (Ed.) *Fourth Survey of Research in Education* (1983-88), Vol. I, New Delhi, NCERT, p. 848.

Samuel W., 1981. *Personality Searching for the Sources of Human Behaviour.* New Delhi: McGraw Hill.

Sarkar, U., 1983. Contribution of some Home Factors on Childrens Scholastic Achievement, Ph.D. Psy., cal. U., cit. In. Buch, M. B. (Ed.) *Fourth Survey of Research in Education.* 1983-88, Vol. I, p. 849, NCERT.

Saun, G.S. , 1980. Patterns of self-disclosure and Adjustment among High and low Achievers. Cit. in Buch. M.B. (Ed.) *Third Survey of Research in Education*, Ph.D Psy, Kum U; pp.686–687 New Delhi, NCERT.

Savage, R. D., 1966. Personality Factors and Academic Attainment in Junior School Children. *The British J. Ed. Psy.*, 36, pp. 91-92.

Sayler, M. F. and Brookshire, W. K., 1993. Social, Emotional and behavioural Adjustment of accelerated students, Students in Gifted classes and Regular Students in Eighty Grade. *Gifted Child Quarterly*, Vol. 37, No. 4, pp. 148-154.

Scott, M. S. et al., 1996. Identifying cognitively Gifted Ethnic Minority Children. *Gifted Child Quarterly*, Vol. 40, No. 3, pp. 147-153.

Seers, R. R., 1977. Sources of life Satisfactions of the Terman Gifted Men. *American Psychologist.* Vol. 32, No. 2, PP. 119-128.

Seethi, V. K., 1990. Personality patterns of High Achieving and Low Achieving Students in Professional Courses. *Indian Educational Review*, Vol. 25, No. 1, Jan. pp. 92-94.

Sen Barat, Kalpana, 1992. An investigation into the personality make up, intelligence and study habit of high and low Achievers. Ph.D. Edu. Univ. of Calcutta. *Fifth*

Survey of Research in education, 1988-92, Vol. I, p. 724, NCERT, New Delhi.

Shah, A. R. , 1977. Need Achievement as a Function of Personality, M.Ed. Dissertation, Kashmir University Lib.

Shah, C. Z., 1969. A Study of the superior children in the state of Gujrat, Ph.D. Edu. MSU. Cit. In Buch, M. B. (Ed.). *First Survey of Research in Education.*

Shah, J. H., 1990. A study of relationship among intelligence, self-concept and academic achievement of pupils of standard X of semi-urban and rural areas of Sihore Taluka, *Experiments in Education*, Vol. XVII (4), 104-110 cit in. *Fifty Survey of Research in Education.* 1988-92, Vol. I, p. 724. NCERT, New Delhi.

Sharma, K. G., 1972. A comparative study of adjustment of over and Underachievers. Ph.D. Thesis in Education, Allahabad University cit. In Hota, N. (1986) School Achievement and Personality: A TAT Study. *Indian J. of Psy.* Pp. 42-51.

Sharma, Premalata, 1981. A study of Factors related to Academic Under achievement of Girls of secondary schools located in rural areas of Haryana Ph.D (Edu. Mys .U; cit. in Buch, M. B. (Ed) *Fourth Survey of Research in Education*, Vol. I, New Delhi; p.851, NCERT.

Shaw, M.C., 1964. Definition and Identification of Academic Underachievers. Cit. In, French, J. L. (Ed.) *Educating the Gifted.* Pp. 325-340. New York: Holt, Rinehart and Winston, INC.

Shivapa, D., 1980. Factors affecting the Academic Achievement of High School Pupils, Ph.D. Edu. Kar. U., cit. In: Third Survey of Research in Education 1978-83. P. 690, NCERT.

Silverman, L. K., 1991. *Family Counselling in Handbook of the Gifted Education* by N. Colangelo and G. Dabvis (eds.) Allyn and Bacon.

Singh, B. , 1986. A study of some possible contributing Factors to high and low achievement in Mathematics of the School students of Orissa Ph.D, (Ed) cit. in, Buch,

M.B (Ed.) *Fourth Survey of Research in Education.* Vol I, New Delhi; NCERT, p. 854.

Singh, B.. , 1986. A study of some possible contributing Factors to high and low achievement in Mathematics of the High School students of Orissa. Ph.D. Edu. Cit. In Buch., M.B. (Ed.) *Fourth Survey of Research in Education.* Vol. New Delhi: NCERT, P. 854.

Singh, K., 1987. Academic Achievement as a function of creative thinking and intelligence among High School students of Himachal Pradesh, *J. of Institute of educational Research,* Vol. II, No. 1, Jan.

Singh, K., 1987. Academic Achievement as a function of creative thinking and intelligence among high school students of Himachal Pradesh. *J. of Institute of Educational Research.* Vol. II .No- I Jan.

Singh, R. P., 1983. Under and over-achievement and its Motivational correlates (A Factor Analytical Study). Ph.D., Psy. Cit. In, Buch M. B. (Ed.) *Fourth Survey of Research in Education.* Vol. 1, New Delhi, NCERT, P. 856.

Sinha, D., 1970. *Academic Achievers and Non-Achievers* Allahabad: United Publishers.

Sinha, N.C.P., 1976. Need for Achievement and Academic Attainment. *Indian Educational Review.* Vol. 5, No. 2., July.

Sinha, S., et al., 1988. Scholastic Achievement: A Study of High and Low Achievers with special reference to their intelligence and Family Variables. *Ind. J. Clin. Psychol., 15: pp. 103-107.*

Somasundaram, M., 1980. *A comparative study of certain personality variable related to over – normal and underachievement in secondary school Mathematics,* Ph.D. Edu; Calicut.

Sontakey, V. V., 1986. A comparative study of Personality Factors and Achievement Motivation of High and Low Achievers in Natural and Biological Sciences. Ph.D. Edu. Cit. In, Buch, M. B. (Ed.) *Fourth Survey of Research in*

Education (1983-88), Vol. I, New Delhi, NCERT, PP. 858-59.

Sontaky, G.R., 1975. An experimental study of bright underachieving boys. Scientia Paedagogica Experimentals, 12(1), pp.221-247 cit. In: Maitra Krishna, *Gifted Underachievers–A challenge in Education.* New Delhi. Discovery Publishing House, 1991. p. 48.

Srivastava, G. P., 1978. Development of a socio-economic status scale. The *Ind. J. of Social Work*, Vol. XXXIX. No. 2, pp. 133-138.

Stagner, R., 1961. *Psychology of Personality* (Rev. Ed.) New York: McGraw Hill.

Stanley J. C., 1976. Accelerating the Educational Progress of Intellectually Gifted Children. Cit. In., Dennis, W. and Dennis, M. W. (Eds.) *The Intellectually Gifted: An Overview.* New York, Gurne and Stratton. 179-196.

Stephens, J. M., 1960. *Educational Psychology.* New York: Holt, Rinehart and Winston, P. 172.

Sternberg, R. J., 1985. Beyond IQ: A triarchic Theory of Human Intelligence. New York, Cambridge University Press.

Sternberg, R. J., 1986. *Intelligence Applied: Understanding and Increasing your Intellectual Skills.* San Diego: Harcourt, Brace, Javanovich.

Sternberg, R. J. and Clinkenbeard P., 1995. Triarchic View of Identifying, Teaching and Assessing Gifted Children. *Roeper Review,* 17, 255-260.

Sternberg, R. J. et al., 1996. Identification, Instruction, Assessment of Gifted Children: A Construct Validation of Triarchic Model. *Gifted Child Quarterly,* Vol. 40, No. 3, pp. 129-137.

Strang, R., 1951, *Mental hygiene of gifted children* I.N.P witty (Ed.) the gifted child. Lexington, Mass: D.C Health.

Strang, R., 1956, Gifted Adolescents Views of Growing up. *Exceptional Children,* 23, pp. 10-15.

Strong, J. H., and et al., 1987. Educating the culturally Disadvantaged, Gifted students. *The School Counsellor, Vol. 34, No. 5, PP. 336-344.*

Sumption, M. R. and Evelyn, M., 1960. *Education of the Gifted.* New: Ronald Press Co.

Sween, 1984. Academic Achievement of High school students in Relation to the Instructional Design, Intelligence, Self-concept and n-achievement, Ph.D. Edu. Pan. U; cit. in Buch, M.B. (Ed) *Fourth Survey of Research in Education* 1983-88, Vol. I, p. 861

Swensson, O.K., 1986, Classroom behaviours of Male Academically Gifted Underachievers, Academically Gifted Achievers and Average Students. A comparatiye study *Dissertation Abstract International*, Vol. 47, No. 06, Dec.

Swiateu, M. A., 2001, Social coping among Gifted high school students and its relationship to self-concept. *Journal of Youth and Adolescence*, 30, 19-39.

Taylor, R. G., 1964, Personality traits and Discrepant Achievement: A Review. *J. of Counselling Pschology*, 11, 76-82.

Terman, L.M., 1917, The Intelligence quotient of Francis Galton in Childhood. *Amer. J. Psy.*, 28, pp. 209-215.

Terman L.M and Oden, M .H:, 1947, *The gifted child grows up in genetic studies of genius*, Vol. II, Stanford Univ. Press, Stranford.

Terman, L. M. et al., 1926, Mental and Physical Traits of a Thousand Gifted Children, *Genetic Studies of Genius*, Vol. I. Stanford Univ. Press.

Tewari, D. D. and Rai, P.N., 1976, Some Differential Personality Correlates of low and High Achievers. *Indian Educational Review*, Vol. 11, No. 2, April. Pp. 70-82.

Thomson, A. K., 1986, Depression and underachievement in the Gifted Male Adolescents. *Dissertation Abstract International*, Vol. 47, No. 06 pp. 2093-A to 2094-A.

Travers, R. M. W., 1978, *An Introduction to Educational Research*, 4th Ed., New York: Macmillan Publishing Co., Inc.

References

Treffinger, D. J., 1991, School Reform and Gifted Education - Opportunities and Issues. *Gifted Child Quarterly,* Vol. 35, No. 1, P. 61-11.

Tripathy, P. K. and Misra, C.H.K., 1984, *Status of Gifted children Experience in Indian context. A trend Report.* Report of the National Seminar on Identification and Development of gifted children. 10-12 NIPCO, New Delhi - 110016, pp 2-16.

Tuckman, B. W , 1972, *Conducting Educational Research.* New York: Harcout Brace, Jovanovich Incharge.

Tyler, L. E., 1965. *The Psychology of Human Differences* (3rd ed.,) Bombay: Vikas Feffer and Simons Pvt.

Urban, K K., '1991. Giftedness and Behavioural Disorders. *International J. of Special Education,* Vol. 6, No. 1, pp. 12-27.

Vaghn, V. L. and et al., 1991. Meta analysis and Review of Research on Pullout Programmes in Gifted Edu., *Gifted Child Quarterly,* Vol. 35, No. 2, pp. 92-98.

Van Dalen, D.B., 1973. *Understanding Educational Research* (3rd Ed.) New York: McGraw Hill Book .Co.

Vantassel Baska, J., 1991. Gifted Education in the Balance: Building Relationships with General Education. *Gifted Child Quarterly,* Vol. 35, No. 1, PP. 20-25.

Vashishtha, U. C., 1980. Importance and Role of Gifted in Society. *J. Indian Edu.,* Vol. 10, Aug. pp. 16-18.

Verma, R. M. , 1962. Development of a tool to apprise Socio-economic Status. *J. Psychol Res*; 6, pp. 35-38

Vernon, P. E., 1951. *The structure of human abilities.* New York: John Wiley.

Vespi L. and Yewchuk, C., 1991, Socio-emotional characteristics of Gifted Learning Disabled Children. *International Journal of Special Education,* Vol. 6, No. 1.

Waddington, M and Obrien , G., 1979. *Promise Unfolding,* London: NAGC.

Walia, D., 1973, *The Gifted Adolescent and their self-concepts.* Ph.D. thesis. Punjab U.

Webb, J. T. et al., 1982. *Guiding the Gifted Child: A Practical Source for Parents and Teachers,* Columbus, Ohio Psychology Publishing Company.

Whitemore Joanne Rand, 1980. *Giftedness Conflict and Under-achievement.* Boston: Allyn and Bacon Inc.

Wilgosh, L., 1991. Underachievement and Related Issues for culturally Different Gifted children. International *J. of Special Edu*; Vol.6, No.1, pp.82-87.

Witly, P. A., 1958. Who are the gifted? In N.B. Henry (Ed.) The Fifty Seventh Year Book of the National Society of Education, Part II; *Education of the Gifted.* Chicago: University of Chicago Press.

Witty, P. A. and Lehman, H. C., 1929. Nervous instability and genius Poetry and Fiction. *J. Abnorm. Soc. Psychol.*, 24, 77-90.

Witty, P. A. and Lehman, H. C., 1930. Nervous instability and genius. Some conflicting opinions. *J. Abnorm. Soc. Pychol.,* 24. 468-497.

Wright, S., 1955. Some Psychological and Physiological correlates of certain academic Underachievers. Ph.D. thesis., University of Chicago Library cit. In Cattell R. B and Cattell M.D.L. *Handbook for the Jr.-Sr. HSPQ*< New Delhi: Psycho-Centre.

Yates, P.H., 1975. The relationship between self concept and academic achievement among gifted elementary school students. *Dissertation Abstract International* 36, 2665-A.

Yearbook, 1958. *Education for the Gifted,* Fifty seventh yearbook of the National Society for the Study of Education., Part II. Chicago University of Chicago Press, P. 19.

Zilli, M. J., 1971. Reasons why Gifted adolescent Underachievers and some of the implications of guidance and counseling to this problem. *Gifted Child Quarterly,* 15, pp. 279-292.

Index

Author Index

Subject Index

Index